Tamplen Family Cookbook

Brian K. Tamplen

Frankie Ann Tamplen

Contents

Appetizers

Beverages

Breads

Breakfast

Desserts

Entrees

Salads

Soups

Other

All rights to this cookbook are reserved by Brian K. Tamplen & Frankie A. Tamplen

Message from the Authors

JANUARY 28, 2024

Dear reader,

Thank you for reading our family cookbook. Inspired by love and family traditions, these recipes have been handed down from generations. Recipes were contributed from Tamplen family members with love. Enjoy the journey instead of the result.

We've tried to include family pictures that detail our lives and journeys. Life is short. Enjoy the ride. Embrace your family.

Sincerely,

Brian K. Tamplen & Frankie A. Tamplen

Where it all began. Between 1996 and 1998 my wife had a great idea to create a family cookbook from her family – the Spicer's. I loved the idea so much I collected the Tamplen family recipes and typed in the recipes into a program called Legacy which also housed all of my genealogy research. From that program, I printed out personally labeled copies of the Tamplen family cookbook and Addie bound them by hand. I then mailed those out to our family members. If you received a copy of this cookbook, you have a very rare version indeed. We probably only printed and bound about 30 copies. Technology is a wonderful thing and I can now enter the recipes into Word and publish via Amazon in a few keystrokes and anyone can get a copy at a reasonable price from all over the world.

Below is a picture of what the originals looked like way back in 1998!

Dave & Lexie Tamplen are my paternal grandparents and Maggie Tamplen is my paternal great-grandmother.

During my genealogy research, I found that the Tamplen name is derived from the Tamplin surname. Stories abound about how this occurred (two brothers fighting/disagreeing, banking information getting mis-written before everyone knew how to read and write, etc.). We may never know the full truth. Doesn't matter – we are all family. Using my genealogy contacts, I was able to get a few Tamplin family member recipes!

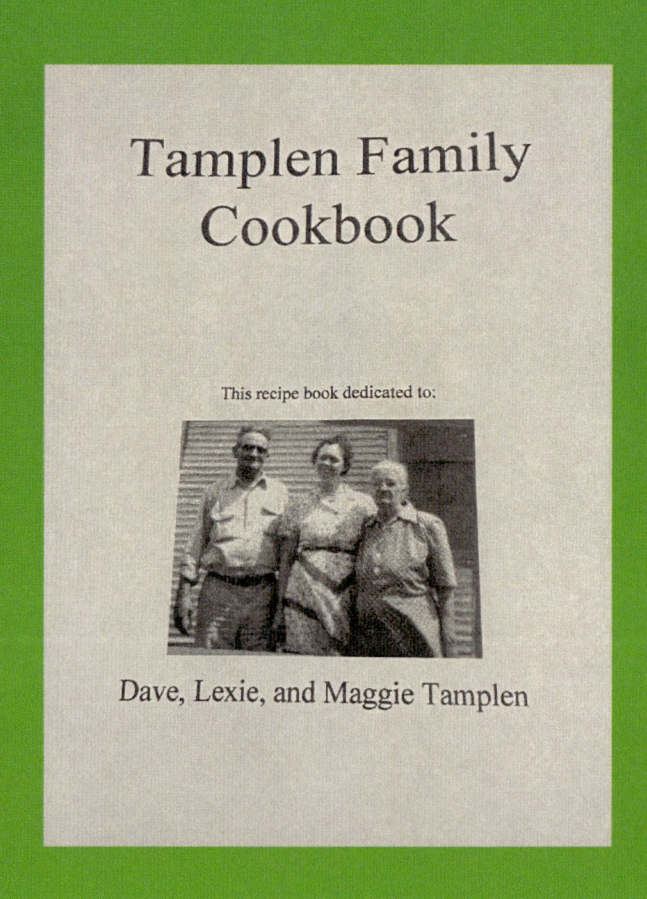

APPETIZERS

Cheese Fondue

Addie Ann Spicer Tamplen

Addie Ann Spicer and Max

INGREDIENTS

1 ½ cups milk
2 – 8-ounce pack cream cheese, softened
½ teaspoon salt
2 ½ ounces parmesan cheese, grated

STEPS

On low heat mix cream cheese and milk stirring until smooth and hot.

Add parmesan cheese and salt.

Makes 4 servings.

Cranberry Pecan Goat Cheese Truffles

Dewayne and Kris Tamplen

INGREDIENTS

10 oz goat cheese
6 oz cream cheese
2 tsp cinnamon
3 tbsp honey, plus extra for garnish
1 1/2 cups pecan chips - divided
1 C diced dried cranberries
1/2 cup minced fresh parsley

STEPS

In a lg bowl, beat together the goat cheese, cream cheese, cinnamon and honey until light and fluffy. Add 1/2 cup pecan chips folding to combine. Set aside.

Line your countertop with parchment paper. Toss together remaining pecan chips, dried cranberries and parsley in the center of the parchment paper.

Using a lg cookie scoop, scoop out one round of cheese filling and toss in the cranberry pecan mixture. Continue until all truffles have been rolled in coating.

Refrigerate cheeseballs until ready to serve. You can make these up to 3 days before, just make sure and store them in an airtight container in the refrigerator.

To serve: Drizzle truffles with honey, if desired. Serve with crackers, warm crostini or as is with a toothpick (or pretzel stick)

Fiesta Stack-Ups

Dewayne and Kris Tamplen

INGREDIENTS/STEPS

Meat Sauce:
4 lbs lean ground beef
3 lg onions chopped
2 (14 oz) cans whole tomatoes
2 (15 oz) cans tomato sauce
2 (12 oz) cans tomato puree'
4 T chili powder
2 tsp cumin
1 tsp garlic powder
6 tsp salt
2 (23 oz) cans ranch style beans

Brown beef and onions; drain excess fat. Add remaining ingredients except beans. Simmer uncovered 1-1 1/2 hours. Add beans and heat thoroughly.

Serve buffet style in the following order:

2 (12 oz) pkg crushed Fritos
1 (14 oz) box of rice (cooked)
Meat sauce
2 lbs cheddar cheese (grated)
2 lg onions (chopped)
1 (4 1/2 oz) can ripe olives (pitted and chopped)
1 C chopped pecans
1 (7oz) pkg coconut
1 (16oz) jar picante sauce

Be sure to use ALL ingredients. The sweet taste of the coconut and pecans really makes this a treat.

Will serve 20 hungry people.

*On a side note, I do not like coconut, but just a little with this combination makes it!!

1 ½ cups milk
2 – 8-ounce pack cream cheese, softened
½ teaspoon salt
2 ½ ounces parmesan cheese, grated

Harold, Frankie, Dewayne, and Brian Tamplen

Hearty Black Bean Quesadillas

Dewayne and Kris Tamplen

INGREDIENTS

1 (15 oz) can black beans
1 cup frozen corn (or can use can)
1/2 C red onion
1 clove garlic
1/4 bunch fresh cilantro (about 1/2 cup chopped)
2 C shredded cheddar cheese
1 pkg taco seasoning
10 flour tortillas (7 in. diameter)

STEPS

Drain the black beans and add them to a bowl along with the corn (no need to thaw)

Finely dice the onion, mince the garlic, and roughly chop the cilantro.

Add the onion, garlic, cilantro, shredded cheddar cheese, and taco seasoning to the bowl with the beans and corn. Stir until everything is evenly combined and coated in seasoning.

Place 1/2 cup of the filling on one side of each tortilla and fold over. Cook the quesadillas in a skillet over medium heat on each side until brown and crispy and the cheesy filling has melted.

To freeze the quesadillas, stack the filled and uncooked quesadillas with a piece of parchment paper between each quesadilla. Place in a freezer bag and freeze for. up to 3 months. To reheat either microwave (for a soft quesadilla) or cook in a skillet on low heat (make sure to use low heat so that the filling has time to thaw and melt before the outside burns).

Bailey, Corbin, and Tyler Tamplen

Pepper/Cabbage Relish

Frankie A. Tamplen

Harold and Frankie Ann Tamplen

INGREDIENTS

¾ cup white vinegar
¾ cup water
2 teaspoons salt
1/3 cup granulated sugar
1 tablespoon mustard seed
6 cups shredded green cabbage
1 cup diced sweet pepper
2 4-ounce cans pimentos, cut into ¾ inch cubes
1 red onion, thinly sliced

STEPS

In medium saucepan combine vinegar, water, salt, sugar, and mustard seed. Bring to a boil, then simmer five minutes; cool until warm.
In large bowl combine cabbage, pepper, pimentos, and onion. Pour on marinade then toss. Refrigerate tightly covered tossing occasionally. Best when it sets overnight.
This is a pretty dish for Christmas.

Lexie, Dave, Davis Roy, Harold, and Jack Tamplen

Pepperidge Farm party rolls

Frankie A. Tamplen

The Tamplen Family

INGREDIENTS

2 cans Hormel Chunk Ham
1 package Kraft Garlic Cheese (softened)
¼ Bell Pepper, chopped
4 Green Onions, chopped fine
3 drops Tabasco sauce
3 drops Worcestershire sauce
¾ cup Miracle Whip
2 packages Pepperidge Farm Rolls

STEPS

Mix together ham and garlic cheese.

Add bell pepper and green onions, Tabasco sauce, and Worcestershire sauce. Add Miracle Whip. Refrigerate overnight.

Remove a small sliver out of the middle of each roll and put a small portion of ham mixture inside and bake at 325 degrees for 5 to 8 minutes.

Makes 60 rolls.

Harold, Charles, Jack, Ann (Andrew Jackson Jr's wife), Dave, and Ralph Tamplen

Sausage Cheese Balls

Brian K. Tamplen

Frankie, Harold, and Dewayne Tamplen

INGREDIENTS

3 cups Bisquick baking mix
Milk
10 ounces sharp cheddar cheese
1 pound sausage – mild or hot

STEPS

Put Bisquick mix in large bowl. Add just enough milk to make the dough stick together. Add grated cheese and sausage. Mix all ingredients well, roll into small balls and bake at 350 degrees F until brown.
   Makes 20 servings.

Sausage Cheese Balls

Frankie A. Tamplen

Dewayne, Randy, Frankie Ann, Harold, and Brian Tamplen

INGREDIENTS

1 ¾ pounds sausage, uncooked
3 cups Bisquick baking mix
8 ounces grated cheddar cheese

STEPS

Mix all ingredients together and shape into balls.

Bake at 350 degrees for 15 to 20 minutes.

These freeze well. You can take them out of the freezer and bake as many as you need at a time.

Makes 20 servings.

Sausage Cresent Bites

Dewayne and Kris Tamplen

INGREDIENTS

1/2 lb ground sausage (cooked and drained)
1/2 tsp onion powder
1/2 tsp salt
1/2 tsp ground pepper
4 oz cream cheese (softened)
1/4 cup dried cranberries (finely minced)
2 Tbsp pickled Jalapeno peppers
2 cans Pillsbury Crescent Rolls (better if you can find the flat sheets rather than the perforated ones for rolls)

STEPS

Brown the sausage in a lg. skillet breaking it up into small pieces. As the ground sausage cooks, add the onion powder, salt and pepper. Once all the sausage is no longer pink and is cooked through, drain the cooked ground sausage well in a colander. Set aside to cool.

While the sausage is cooling, preheat the oven to 375. and prepare the crescent roll dough.
Cut parchment paper about 12x16 and lay one piece down on the counter or cutting board.

Open crescent roll packaging and place the starting end 2 inches from one edge of parchment paper.
(If using the perforated dough) Unroll the dough carefully without splitting the perforated edges of the crescent roll dough. Pinch seams together sealing the dough back together.

Place a piece of parchment paper over the top and rub your hand over it to smooth it out. With a rolling pin, roll the dough into a 12x8 rectangle (if using perforated dough).

Flip parchment covered dough over without disturbing and gently roll the pin over the opposite side of dough.

Slide the dough (with parchment paper) onto a cookie sheet and chill in the refrigerator for 10 min.. Repeat with other Crescent rolls.

After about 10 min. remove one baking sheet of dough from the refrigerator and place it on your work surface. Peel the top parchment paper off.

Trim the edges with a sharp knife so they are even.

With a sharp knife, cut into 6 rows by 4 rows to make 24 squares. Set aside.

FILLING:
Place the cream cheese, minced dried cranberries, and roughly chopped pickled jalapeno peppers into a small mixing bowl. Mix until combined.

Using a teaspoon, scoop the filling in the center of each square of crescent roll dough.

Gently pick up a square of crescent dough trying not to stretch dough and bring two opposite corners together.

Pinch the dough together and twist so it sticks together.

Place the filled sausage crescent bites on the lined baking sheet. Repeat with all of the squares of crescent dough leaving about 2 inches between each appetizer on the baking sheet.

Once the baking sheet is filled or you have made all the appetizers bake in the preheated oven for 10-14 min. until golden.

Krista, Makai, Georges Tenie, and Corbin Tamplen

Seven Layer Dip

Brian K. Tamplen

Addie Ann Spicer and Brian Tamplen

INGREDIENTS

1 bunch cilantro
2 cans bean dip
2 avocados
2 tomatoes
1 head iceberg lettuce
½ pint sour cream
½ cup Miracle Whip
1 package taco seasoning
Grated American Cheese

STEPS

Chop ingredients as necessary and layer into a 9x12 inch pan. Spread cheese on top.

Makes 8 servings.

Houston, Floyd, Leon, and Andrew Jackson Tamplen, Jr.

Taco Roll-ups

Frankie A. Tamplen

INGREDIENTS

2 pounds ground chuck
2 medium onions
4 – 6 jalapeno peppers
1 can refried beans
2 packages Lowry's Taco Mix or Old El Paso taco seasoning mix
1 package flour tortillas
1 small can ripe olives
1 package of finely shredded mild cheddar cheese

STEPS

Chop onions and peppers and put in skillet with meat and cook until meat is brown. Drain. Mix in one can refried beans.

Soak 2 packages of Lowry's Taco Mix with 1 cup warm water for 10 minutes.

Mix with beans and meat mixture. Let simmer until thick.

Roll in tortillas and cheese and chopped ripe olives.

Harold Tamplen

Thai Chicken Lettuce Wraps

Dewayne and Kris Tamplen

INGREDIENTS

1 Tbsp olive oil (or vegetable or canola oil)
1 lb ground chicken
4 cloves garlic, minced
1/2 tsp salt
1/4 tsp freshly ground black pepper
1 C carrot, shredded
1/2 C finely shredded cabbage
3 green onions

For the sauce:
1/4 C fresh cilantro, chopped
1/3 C sweet chili sauce (found in the Asian section of grocery store)
1 Tbsp chunky (or smooth) peanut butter
1/4 tsp freshly grated ginger
2 tsp low sodium soy sauce
Crushed red pepper flakes, to taste
Boston Bib lettuce, or romaine lettuce leaves

STEPS

Heat oil in lg skillet over medium heat. Add chicken, garlic, onions, salt and pepper and cook, stirring occasionally, until chicken is cooked through.

Add the carrots, cabbage, and green onions, cooking an additional 4-5 minutes or until vegetables are tender.

In a small bowl, combine the sweet chili sauce, ginger, peanut butter, and soy sauce, and crushed red pepper. Stir until smooth. Add to pan along with chopped cilantro. Stir to coat.

Spoon mixture into lettuce leaves and enjoy.

* can substitute ground turkey

Vegetable Spring Rolls

Addie Ann Spicer Tamplen

INGREDIENTS

6 rice paper (Asian food stores)
2 cups rice noodles – boiled in water, drained and cooled
1 cup red bell pepper, carrot, cucumber mix, thinly sliced
1 cup celery, yellow bell pepper, jicama mix, thinly sliced
1 cup zucchini, yellow squash mix, thinly sliced
6 leaves Boston lettuce, ½ leaf per paper
6 leaves Radicchio lettuce - tear away center
1 tablespoon cilantro, chopped
Mint
Basil

STEPS

Dip rice paper sheets in hot water until pliable. If rice paper is too soft, it will easily tear. Hang paper over bowl while preparing others. Lay the rice paper on lightly moistened stainless steel surface. Place a leaf of Radicchio and Boston leaf in center of rice paper. Place a few tablespoons of the vegetables in rows atop the lettuces. Place ¼ cup of rice noodles on top of vegetable and sprinkle with cilantro, basil, and mint. Roll the rice paper to make a cigar shaped spring roll. Cover with damp cloth and refrigerate until ready to serve. Can be kept in fridge 1-2 days.

Serve with red chili pepper vinaigrette.

Can add cooked lobster, shrimp, salmon, tuna, etc.

Makes 6 servings.

BEVERAGES

Brian's Famous Margaritas

Brian K. Tamplen

Brian Tamplen

INGREDIENTS

8 limes well-squeezed
1 cup good tequila
¼ cup Gran Marnier
¾ cup cold water
¼ cup Agave Nectar

STEPS

Mix all ingredients and serve over ice.

This recipe has a great backstory. I was in Las Vegas at Javier's restaurant in the Aria Resort and Casino. I ordered a margarita and was served the best tasting margarita I had ever tasted. I asked the waiter for the recipe. I was told to hold on. The waiter disappeared and brought out Javier himself who told me he wouldn't give me his homemade recipe but he would tell me the ingredients for me to figure it out for myself. I worked hard trying different combinations and came out with this. I hope you enjoy it. And, if you get to Las Vegas please try the original at Javier's in Aria.

Thanks Javier!

Christmas Punch

Brian K. Tamplen

Blizzard and Brian Tamplen

INGREDIENTS

1 12-ounce frozen cranberry juice
1 12-ounce frozen orange juice
1 12-ounce frozen pineapple juice (or large can)
3 whole lemons, juiced and seeded

STEPS

Mix all juices with correct amount of water and mix well together. Add lemon juice.

Enjoy hot or cold!

Hot Chocolate Mix

Frankie A. Tamplen

Dewayne, Harold, and Brian Tamplen

INGREDIENTS

1 large can Nestle Quick Chocolate Instant mix (2 lbs)
1 large jar coffee creamer
1 medium box instant powdered milk
1 pound powdered sugar
Cocoa to taste

STEPS

Mix all ingredients.

Use 3 - 4 tablespoons per cup of hot water.

Makes 50 servings.

Charles, Dave, Jack, and Harold Tamplen

Spice Tea Mix

Addie Ann Spicer Tamplen

INGREDIENTS

2 cups Tang
½ cup Instant Tea
1 cup sugar (if tea is unsweetened)
1 small pack lemon and mix – if tea is lemonless
1 large box apricot/orange Jello
1 package Red Hots
1 teaspoon cinnamon
1 teaspoon ground cloves

STEPS

Mix all ingredients.

Use 2 – 3 teaspoons per cup of hot water.

Brian Tamplen

BREADS

Creole Corn Muffins

Addie Ann Spicer Tamplen

INGREDIENTS

2 eggs, well beaten
1 ½ cups milk
¾ cup shortening, melted
2 tablespoons chopped green Bell pepper
2 tablespoons chopped onion
2 tablespoons chopped pimento
¾ cup grated American cheese
2 ½ cups flour
1 teaspoon salt
2 tablespoons baking powder
4 tablespoons plus 1 teaspoon sugar
4 tablespoons plus 1 teaspoon cornmeal

STEPS

Mix eggs, milk, and shortening. Add green pepper, onion, pimento, and cheese to flour, salt, baking powder, sugar, and cornmeal. Add the milk mixture and stir only enough to mix.

Bake at 400 degrees F for 25 – 30 minutes.

Makes 6 servings.

Indian Bread

Brian K. Tamplen

Dewayne, Randy, and Brian Tamplen

INGREDIENTS

½ cup sifted flour
1 ½ cups yellow cornmeal
½ teaspoon salt
4 tablespoons sugar
2 eggs, beaten well
1 cup sour cream
1 teaspoon baking soda
1 ½ cups milk

STEPS

Preheat oven to 400 degrees F. Combine flour, cornmeal, salt, and sugar in a bowl. Add the eggs and sour cream and beat until very smooth. Dissolve the baking soda in the milk. Add to the previous mixture and stir well. Pour into a battered nine-inch loaf pan.

Bake in 400 degree F oven for 25 minutes or until a cake tester comes out clean and the bread is slightly browned.

Makes 8 servings.

Lexie Mae and Davis Roy Tamplen

Scalloped Corn

Mike and Sandra Tamplen Highland

Mike and Sandra Tamplen Highland

INGREDIENTS

1 box Jiffy Corn Bread mix
1 can cream corn
1 can whole kernel corn, drained
¾ cup sour cream
1 stick margarine
½ cup milk
1 egg

STEPS

Mix together all ingredients and bake uncovered in a glass Pyrex bowl for one hour at 350 degrees F.

Makes 4 servings.

Toasted Ranch French Bread

Ralph and Francille Tamplen

Brian K. Tamplen, Francille Tamplen, Frankie Ann Tamplen, Harold Tamplen

INGREDIENTS

2 loaves French bread
1 1-ounce package ranch dressing mix
½ cup butter or margarine, softened

STEPS

Combine ranch dressing mix and butter/margarine.

Slice loaves length wise and spread with butter/ranch dressing mixture.

Cut diagonally into two-inch wedges.

Toast under broiler or toast cut surface down on grill until golden brown.

Serve hot.

Makes 6 servings.

Ralph, Francille, Tani, and Terri Lynn Tamplen

Biscuits

Dewayne and Kris Tamplen

Dewayne Tamplen and Kris Tamplen, Corbin Tamplen, Makai Tenie

INGREDIENTS

1 cup flour
1 tablespoon Baking Powder
1 dash salt
½ cup buttermilk

STEPS

Mix together all ingredients and put on floured surface. Roll out mixture with a roller to desired thickness.

Cut out biscuits.

Put into baking pan that has been buttered and heated first.

Bake about 375 degrees F for approximately 15 minutes. This time will depend upon the thickness of your biscuits. Makes about six biscuits.

Makes 3 servings.

Brian's notes; make the biscuits a bit thicker than in these pictures so that they are fluffy and delicious!

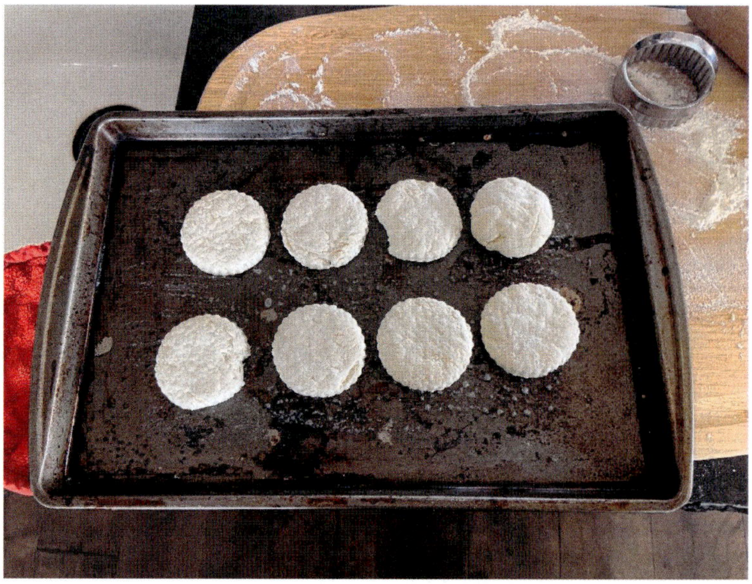

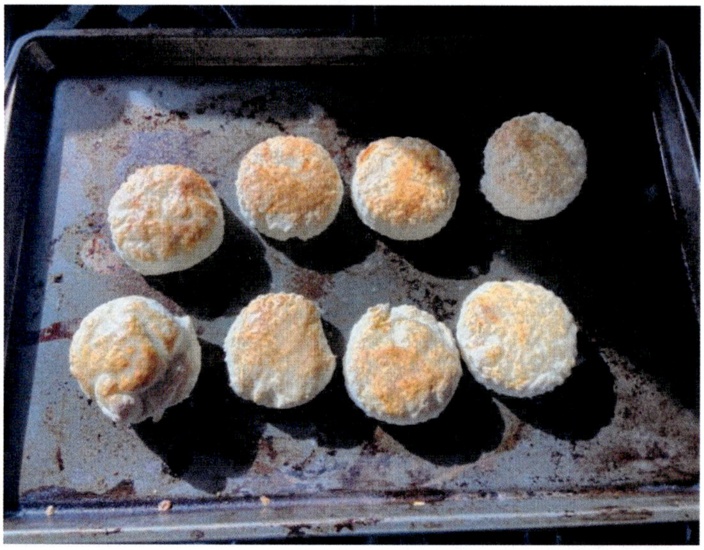

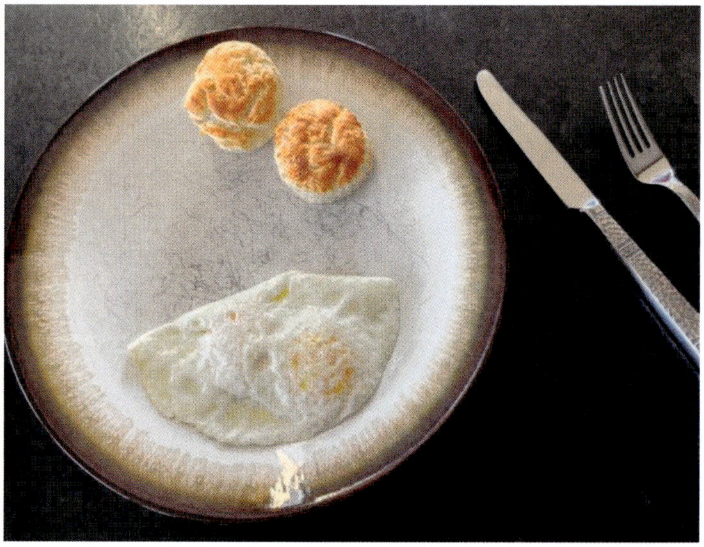

Large Biscuits

Addie Ann Spicer Tamplen

Brian K. Tamplen and Addie Ann Spicer

Lexie Mae Tamplen and Tigger

INGREDIENTS

4 cups flour
4 teaspoons baking powder
1 teaspoon salt
1 teaspoon sugar
¾ cup shortening
1 ¾ cups milk

STEPS

Sift flour.

Add dry ingredients in bowl.

Add shortening and milk and work with hands on board.

Roll out and cut with biscuit cutter.

Bake in a 400 degree F oven for 10 – 12 minutes until brown.

Makes 20 large biscuits.

Makes 10 servings.

Brian Tamplen

DESSERTS

7-Up Cake

Frankie A. Tamplen

Frankie Ann Tamplen and Harold Tamplen

INGREDIENTS

1 box Pineapple cake mix
1 3-ounce instant Pineapple pudding
4 eggs
½ cup vegetable oil
1 10-ounce bottle of 7-Up

7-Up cake icing ingredients
1 ½ cups sugar
2 tablespoons flour
1 stick margarine
2 whole eggs, beaten well
1 20-ounce crushed pineapple
1 small can coconut
1 ½ cups chopped pecans

STEPS

Cake directions.
Mix all ingredients well and bake in three 9-inch pans for 25 – 30 minutes at 325 degrees F. Be sure to grease and flour pans before pouring in batter. Allow to completely cool and remove from pans.

Icing directions.
Mix sugar, flour, margarine, eggs, and crushed pineapple and cook over low heat until thick and then add coconut and chopped pecans.

Spread icing on cake layering as you go along putting each cake on top of the other.

Makes 16 servings.

Harold, Dewayne, and Frankie Tamplen

Addie's Biscotti's

Addie Ann Spicer Tamplen

Addie Ann Spicer and Brian K. Tamplen

Brian Tamplen

INGREDIENTS

1 ½ cups vegetable oil
1 ¾ cups sugar
4 eggs
½ teaspoon salt
2 teaspoons baking powder
4 cups flour
2 cups choice of nuts (almonds or pecans)
1 ounce anise flavor

STEPS

Sift dry ingredients together. Beat sugar and eggs in mixer. Add oil slowly. Continue beating. Add 2/3's of dry mixture and beat until blended. Add remainder of dry mixture and anise. Mix by hand. Add nuts and knead on floured board. Cut into six sections and place on greased cookie sheets. Bake 20 – 25 minutes at 350 degrees F. Cool 2 minutes. Remove to board. Cool another 5 minutes. Slice quickly in ¾ inch size cookie slices. Place back onto cookie sheet. Brown for 15 minutes at 350 degrees F. Be careful not to burn.

Makes 24 servings.

Brian and Addie Ann Spicer Tamplen

Almond Joy Balls

Frankie A. Tamplen

Dewayne, Randy, Brian Tamplen

INGREDIENTS

1 cup white Karo Syrup
2 cups dehydrated coconut
Almonds, toasted
Chocolate almond bark

STEPS

Bring syrup to a bubbling boil but not a rolling boil. Add the dehydrated coconut into syrup and mix well. Let set for 3 hours. Roll enough coconut around one toasted almond to form a ball and then dip into chocolate almond bark that has been melted over a double boiler. Put on wax paper to let chocolate set.

Makes about 50 balls.

                         Makes 25 servings.

Frankie, Brian, and Dewayne Tamplen

Angel Food Cake

Frankie A. Tamplen

INGREDIENTS

1 ¼ cups confectioner's sugar
1 cup cake flour
1 ½ cups egg whites at room temperature (12 – 14 egg whites)
1 ½ teaspoons cream of tartar

1 ½ teaspoons vanilla extract
¼ teaspoon salt
¼ teaspoon almond extract
1 cup sugar

STEPS

Preheat oven to 375 degrees F. In small bowl, stir confectioners' sugar and cake flour; set aside.

Add egg whites, cream of tartar, vanilla extract, salt, and almond extract to large bowl and with mixer at high speed, beat until well mixed.

Beating at high speed, sprinkle in sugar, 2 tablespoons at a time; beat just until sugar dissolves and whites form stiff peaks. Do not scape bowl during beating.

With rubber spatula, fold in flour mixture, about ¼ at a time, just until flour disappear.

Pour mixture into ungreased 10-inch tube pan with spatula cut through batter to break any large air bubbles.

Bake 35 minutes or until top of cake springs back when lightly touched with finger. Any cracks on surface should look dry. Invert cake in pan on funnel; cool completely. With spatula, loosen cake from pan and remove to plate.

Apple Pie

Addie Ann Spicer Tamplen

INGREDIENTS

Crust
2/3 cup plus 2 tablespoons Crisco
2 cups flour
1 teaspoon salt
5 tablespoons cold water

Filling
¾ cup sugar
¼ cup flour
½ teaspoon cinnamon
½ teaspoon nutmeg
Granny Smith apples, peeled and cut

STEPS

Crust:
Cut Crisco and mix with flour and salt until well blended. Add cold water and mix to make soft ball. Roll and line pie pan, reserving enough to top filling.

Filling:
Mix sugar, flour, nutmeg, cinnamon, and apples. Turn into pie pan. Put pats of butter on top. Cover filling with pie crust.

Heat over to 425 degrees F. Bake for 40 – 50 minutes. Cover edge of crust with foil during last 15 minutes to prevent browning.

Makes 8 servings.

Applesauce Cake

Addie Ann Spicer Tamplen

Addie Ann Spicer

INGREDIENTS

1 cup butter
2 cups sugar
3 cups flour
1 cup hot water
2 eggs
2 cups applesauce
2 teaspoons soda
1 cup raisins
1 cup nuts
1 teaspoon nutmeg
1 teaspoon cinnamon
1 teaspoon cloves

Icing
2 cups sugar
1 cup butter
1 cup milk
1 cup raisins
1 cup nuts

STEPS

Cream butter and sugar. Add flour, hot water, eggs, applesauce, and other ingredients. Pour into 1 or 2 buttered loaf pans.

Bake at 350 degrees F for about 1 hour.

Icing:
Cook all ingredients until thick.

Makes 16 servings.

Apricot Bars

Frankie A. Tamplen

Snowball, Randy, Brian, Dewayne Tamplen

INGREDIENTS

1 6-ounce bag dried apricots
½ cup soft margarine
¼ cup granulated sugar
1 1/3 cups flour
½ teaspoon baking powder
¼ teaspoon salt
2 eggs, beaten
1 cup brown sugar
1 ½ cups chopped pecans

STEPS

Rinse apricots – cover with water and boil 10 minutes. Drain, cool, and chop apricots. Set aside.

Heat oven to 350 degrees F. Grease 9x13 inch pan.

Mix margarine, granulated sugar, and 1 cup flour and press into pan and bake 15 to 20 minutes or until lightly brown.

Mix 1/3 cup flour, baking powder, salt, vanilla, nuts, eggs, brown sugar, and apricots. Spread over baked layer.

Bake 30 minutes.

Sprinkle with powdered sugar.

Makes 12 servings.

Banana Pudding

Frankie A. Tamplen

Donnie, Dorothy, and Linda Tamplen

INGREDIENTS

1 cup sugar
¼ cup cornstarch
2 cups millk
3 eggs yolks, beaten well
1 tablespoon butter
1 teaspoon vanilla
3 large bananas
Nabisco Nilla Wafers
1 pinch salt

STEPS

Mix sugar, salt, cornstarch, and milk. Cook over low heat stirring constantly. When it begins to thicken, stir half of mixture into beaten egg yolks. Beat egg mixture into remaining hot mixture and cook 2 minutes longer.

Add butter and vanilla. Layer half the Nilla Wafers and 1 ½ bananas into dish. Pour half of pudding over the Wafers and bananas. Repeat with remaining bananas, Wafers, and pudding. Crumble some Wafers on top.

Best Ever Carrot Cake

Dewayne and Kris Tamplen

Dewayne Tamplen and Tyler Tamplen

INGREDIENTS

2 cups flour
2 cups sugar
2 teaspoons cinnamon
1 teaspoon baking powder
½ teaspoon salt
2 teaspoons baking soda
3 cups grated raw carrots
1 ½ cups vegetable oil
4 eggs
1 teaspoon vanilla

STEPS

Preheat oven to 350 degrees F. Mix the flour, sugar, cinnamon, salt, baking powder, and baking soda.

Stir in carrots.

Add oil, eggs, and vanilla. Blend well. Bake in three 9-inch greased and floured round pans for 30 minutes or until cake tests done. Let cool before icing.

Makes 12 servings.

Dewayne, Randy, Frankie, Harold, and Brian Tamplen

Blueberry Cheesecake Pie

Ralph and Francille Tamplen

Dewayne, Randy, Addie Ann, Brian, Francille, Harold, and Frankie Tamplen

INGREDIENTS

1 envelope unflavored gelatin
½ cup milk
8 ounces cream cheese
2/3 cup sugar
1 teaspoon grated orange peel
½ teaspoon vanilla
1 cup heavy cream (whipped) – can use Cool Whip
1 can blueberry pie filling

STEPS

Sprinkle gelatin over milk in small sauce pan. Dissolve over low heat. Cool to room temperature.

Beat cream cheese with sugar, add grated orange peel and vanilla.

Blend milk/gelatin mixture with mixer on low speed. Fold in whipped cream or Cool Whip.

Chill before eating.

Makes 8 servings.

Ralph and Francille Tamplen

Buckeyes

Frankie A. Tamplen

Frankie Ann Tamplen and Francille Tamplen

INGREDIENTS

1 stick margarine, softened
1 ½ cups creamy peanut butter
1 pound powdered sugar
1 teaspoon vanilla
Almond Bark chocolate

STEPS

Mix all ingredients well. Form into small balls and place on cookie sheet. Refrigerate for 2 – 3 hours. Dip in chocolate leaving a small opening in top for buckeye. Any sweet chocolate may be used to dip buckeyes in.

Makes 36 servings.

Tani and Terri Lynn Tamplen

Caramel Sauce

Sherrie Settle

Dennis Ray Monroe, David Tamplen, Betty Ann Tamplen, Chucky Tamplen

INGREDIENTS

8 ounces cream cheese
¾ cup brown sugar
¼ cup sugar
1 teaspoon vanilla

STEPS

Mix all ingredients and dip with apples (Granny Smith taste the best!).

Makes 8 servings.

Cherry Jello Salad

Frankie A. Tamplen

INGREDIENTS

1 small box cherry Jello – 3 ounces
1 8-ounce carton cottage cheese (small curd)
1 small can crushed pineapple (drained)
1 small can mandarin oranges (drained)
12-ounce Cool Whip
1 cup pecans – chopped

STEPS

Mix Jello and cottage cheese. Add oranges and pineapple (drained).

Add Cool Whip and pecans.

Cool in refrigerator 1 hour before serving.

Keeps for 3 days in refrigerator.

Cherry Pizza

Frankie A. Tamplen

Harold, Frankie, Dewayne, and Brian Tamplen

INGREDIENTS

3 cups red sour cherries, pitted
3 tablespoons cornstarch
1 1/3 cups sugar
½ cup white karo syrup
4 drops red food coloring
1 box Betty Crocker cherry chips cake mix
2 sticks melted butter or margarine
½ cup angel flake coconut
1 ½ cups chopped pecans

STEPS

Grease a 9x13 inch dish. Set aside. Mix well sour cherries, cornstarch, sugar, syrup, and food coloring. Pour this mixture into 9x13 dish. Over this mixture sprinkle cake mix, then melted margarine, then coconut, then chopped pecans.

Bake at 325 degrees F for 1 hour 10 minutes.

Makes 8 servings.

Randy Tamplen

Chocolate Angel Pie

Addie A. Spicer Tamplen

INGREDIENTS

Meringue Shell
3 egg whites
1/8 teaspoon Cream of Tartar
1 dash salt
¾ cup sugar
¾ cup chopped pecans or walnuts
1 teaspoon vanilla

Filling
4 ounces sweet chocolate
3 tablespoons strong coffee (liquid)
1 teaspoon vanilla
1 cup whipping cream, whipped

STEPS

Beat egg whites until foamy. Add Cream of Tartar and pinch of salt and beat until they stand in soft peaks. Add sugar gradually and beat until stiff. Fold in nuts and vanilla. Turn meringue into buttered pie pan and make nestlike shell building up sides ½ inch above edge of pan.

Bake at 325 degrees F for 50 – 55 minutes. Cool

Place chocolate and coffee in pan over low flame. Stir until melted and smooth. Cool and stir in vanilla. Whip the cream and fold in melted chocolate. Turn it into the cooled meringue shell. Chill for at least 2 hours.

Makes 8 servings.

Chocolate Cake Florence

Addie A. Spicer Tamplen

INGREDIENTS

Batter, first phase
4 egg whites
½ cup sugar
2 cups flour, sifted
2 teaspoons baking soda
1 pinch salt

Batter, second phase
½ cup butter
½ cup sugar
4 egg yolks, well beaten

Batter, third phase
4 squares bitter chocolate
1 teaspoon vanilla

Batter, fourth phase
½ cup milk

Icing
4 tablespoons butter
2 cups sugar
½ cup milk
2 squares bitter chocolate
1 teaspoon vanilla
Pecans

STEPS

Batter, first phase
Beat egg whites until stiff. Stir in sugar. Set aside.
In separate bowl, mix sifted flour, baking soda, and salt. Set aside.

Batter, second phase.
Cream butter and add sugar gradually. Blend until creamy. Stir in well beaten egg yolks.

Batter, third phase.
Melt bitter chocolate. Add vanilla extract. Stir into phase two mixture.

Batter, fourth phase.
Add flour mixture (phase one) into butter mixture (phase two) and add milk.

Fold in egg white mixture (phase one) and mix. Pour into buttered pan.

Bake at 350 degrees F for 35 – 40 minutes.

Icing.
Melt butter. Add sugar and milk. Boil, stirring constantly. Reduce heat gradually. Add bitter chocolate. Cook for 10 minutes. Remove heat. Beat to thicken and add vanilla. Add pecans before icing hardens.

Makes 8 servings.

Chocolate Cream Pie (9 inch)

Frankie A. Tamplen

INGREDIENTS

1 ¼ cups of sugar
¼ cup corn starch
¼ teaspoon salt
2 cups milk
3 extra large eggs
1 ½ ounce Baker's Unsweetened Chocolate Bar
1 teaspoon vanilla
2 tablespoons butter

STEPS

Stir into saucepan sugar, salt, cornstarch, and mix in milk.

Cook over medium heat, stirring constantly until mixture begins to thicken.

Slowly stir half of hit mixture into (3) beaten egg yolks.

Return this mixture to the remaining hot mixture and boil for 2 minutes until thick, stirring constantly.

Remove from heat. Add butter, chocolate bar, and vanilla.

Pour into a 9-inch baked pie crust.

Top with meringue.

Meringue
3 extra large egg whites
6 tablespoons sugar
¼ teaspoon cream of tartar

Beat egg whites and cream of tartar until foamy. Beat in sugar, 1 tablespoon at a time. Continue beating until stiff and glossy. DO NOT under beat.

Heap meringue onto hot pie filling and spread over filling, carefully sealing meringue to edge of crust to prevent shrinking and weeping.

Bake at 295 degrees for 40 to 45 minutes until lite brown.

Turn off oven and open door ajar for 10 minutes.

Remove from oven to cool, away from any drafts.

David Jr, Charles, Davis Roy, Jack, Ralph, and Harold Tamplen

Chocolate Delight

Frankie A. Tamplen

Floyd Tamplen

INGREDIENTS

1 cup flour
1 cup pecans, chopped
1 stick margarine, melted

8 ounces cream cheese
1 cup powered sugar
1 cup Cool Whip

1 small box instant vanilla pudding
1 small box instant chocolate pudding
3 cups milk

STEPS

Mix flour, pecans, and margarine well.

Press into oblong pan 7x12 inches and bake at 350 degrees F for 25 to 30 minutes. Cool completely.

Cream cheese, powdered sugar, and cool whip. Mix well and spread on crust. Then mix vanilla pudding, instant chocolate pudding, and milk together.

Beat milk and pudding until thick and spread on cream cheese mixture.

Top with the rest of the Cool Whip and top with a few chopped pecans.

   Makes 8 servings.

Chocolate Pecan Pie

Addie A. Spicer Tamplen

INGREDIENTS

3 eggs, slightly beaten
4 squares semisweet chocolate, melted and cooled
1/3 cup sugar
1 teaspoon vanilla
1 cup karo syrup, light or dark
2 tablespoons butter, melted
1 ½ cups pecan halves
9 inch unbaked pie shell

STEPS

In a large bowl stir eggs, karo syrup, chocolate, sugar, butter, and vanilla until well blended. Stir in pecans. Pour into pie shell.

Bake at 350 degrees F 50 to 60 minutes.

Cool.

    Makes 8 servings.

Chow Mein Noodle Cookies

Frankie A. Tamplen

Corbin Tamplen

INGREDIENTS

6 ounces chocolate chips
6 ounces butterscotch chips
1 can Chow Mein noodles
1 cup chopped pecans

STEPS

Melt chips in double broiler. Add noodles and pecans. Drop by teaspoonful on waxed paper.

Makes 12 servings.

Harold Tamplen

Coconut Cream Pie 9-inch

Frankie A. Tamplen

Charles Tamplen and Frankie Ann Tamplen

INGREDIENTS

1 cup sugar
¼ cup cornstarch
¼ teaspoon salt
2 cups milk
3 egg yolks, beaten
1 teaspoon vanilla
2 tablespoons margarine
1 small can angel flake coconut

STEPS

Cook crust and let cool

In a saucepan cook sugar, cornstarch, salt, and milk over low heat, stirring constantly, until the mixture begins to thicken. Stir half of the mixture into the beaten egg yolks. Beat egg mixture into remaining hot mixture and cook 2 minutes. Add vanilla, margarine, and coconut.

Pour into baked pie crust and top with meringue. Sprinkle coconut on top of meringue and put into 295 degree F oven for 40 to 45 minutes. Then turn off oven, open door, and pull the oven rack out a little and let pie sit for 10 minutes. Remove from oven and let cool.

Makes 8 servings.

Coconut Cream Pie 11-inch

Frankie A. Tamplen

INGREDIENTS

1 ½ cups sugar
¼ cup + 2 tablespoons cornstarch
¼ teaspoon salt
3 cups milk
4 eggs, separated – jumbo eggs – at room temperature
2 teaspoons vanilla
3 tablespoons butter
2 ½ cups angel flake coconut – 2 cups for the filling, ½ cup for sprinkling on meringue

Meringue
4 egg whites
8 tablespoons sugar
¼ teaspoon cream of tartar

STEPS

In a saucepan, mix sugar, salt, cornstarch, and milk. Cook over low heat stirring constantly until mixture begins to thicken. In a small bowl, beat egg yolks, add ½ of the hot mixture, and stir until all is mixed. Add this egg mixture back into the remaining hot mixture. Cook for 2 minutes.

Add butter, vanilla, and coconut. Mix well. Pour into prebaked pie crust and top with meringue. Bake at 295 degrees for 40 – 45 minutes or until golden brown. Turn off oven and open oven door and leave pie in oven for 10 minutes. Cool away from draft.

Meringue: Beat egg whites and cream of tartar until foamy. Beat in sugar 1 tablespoon at a time. Continue beating until stiff and glossy. Do not over beat. Heap meringue on pie filling carefully. Be sure to spread meringue to edge of crust to prevent shrinking and weeping. Sprinkle coconut on meringue before cooking.

Pie Crust – 11 inch
2 ¼ cups flour
¼ teaspoon salt
¾ cup Crisco
6 tablespoons ice water

Mix flour and salt, add Crisco. Mix with pastry blender until mixture resembles cornmeal. Add ice water and mix. Roll out on floured board to fit an 11-inch pie plate.

Randy, Avery Ann, Marci, and Tad Tamplen

Cream Cheese Frosting

Dewayne and Kris Tamplen

INGREDIENTS

1 8 ounce cream cheese, softened
1 stick butter, softened
1 16 ounce box powdered sugar, sifted
1 teaspoon vanilla
1 cup pecans

STEPS

Cream together the cheese and butter. Add vanilla and pecans (optional). Blend well. Add milk if necessary to spread.

Refrigerate frosted cake.

Tyler, Kris, and Dewayne Tamplen

Divinity

Frankie A. Tamplen

INGREDIENTS

4 cups sugar
1 cup light Karo corn syrup
¾ cup water
3 egg whites, beaten stiffly
1 teaspoon vanilla
2 cups broken nuts

STEPS

Combine sugar, syrup, and water. Place in saucepan over low heat. Stir until sugar is dissolved; cook without stirring to 225 degrees or until a small amount dropped into cold water forms a hard ball. Remove from heat; pour, beating constantly, in a fine stream into stiffly beaten egg whites. Continue beating until mixture holds shape and loses its gloss. Add vanilla and nuts. Drop quickly from tip of spoon onto waxed paper in individual peaks.

Alternate: can be poured into 9x13 inch buttered dish making it easy to cut into squares and wrap in plastic wrap.

Yields 30 pieces.

Easter Egg "Nests"

Dewayne and Kris Tamplen

INGREDIENTS

4-6 Three Musketeers bars
2 Tbs milk
4 C Rice Krispie cereal
1 C shredded coconut
margarine (for hands later)
green food coloring
Jelly Beans

STEPS

Soften 4 or 6 Three Musketeer bars with 2 TBSP of milk over hot water. Remove candy mixture from heat, stirring until smooth. Combine 4 C Rice Krispies cereal and 1 C shredded coconut in bowl. Fold in candy mixture with rubber spatula. Shape into "nests" approx 2 1/2-3" in diameter with margarine on hands. Makes 12 nests. Place on wax paper. Set in refrigerator to chill. Fill with tinted green coconut and jellybeans (and a chocolate bunny)

*Let candy mix cool before forming nests. After a few minutes of cooling (5-10) form into balls. Then let balls cool about 2-3 min before making nests!

Fresh Strawberry Pie for 11-inch tart pan

Frankie A. Tamplen

Harold Tamplen

INGREDIENTS

1 ½ quarts fresh strawberries, sliced
¾ cup + 6 tablespoons mashed strawberries (remaining strawberries will be sliced)
¾ cup + 6 tablespoons sugar
¾ cup + 6 tablespoons water
4 ½ tablespoons cornstarch
Red food coloring

Use Sweet Pie Crust for filling (see recipe).

STEPS

Mix sugar, cornstarch, mased strawberries, and water in saucepan.

Cook over low heat until thick, stirring constantly.

Remove from heat and add 6 drops of red food coloring.

Let cool and fold in remaining sliced strawberries.

Pour into cooled sweet crust (see recipe below).

Toop with real Whipping Cream (16-ounch carton). Whipped with 3 to 4 tablespoons sugar.

Refrigerate.

Sweet Pie Crust for Fresh Strawberry Pie

Ingredients
1/3 cup + 1 ¼ tablespoons Crisco
1/3 cup + 2 tablespoons Fleischmann's stick margarine
1/3 cup + 1 ¼ tablespoons powdered sugar
1 ½ cup + 6 tablespoons flour

Steps
Cream Crisco and margarine and add powdered sugar and flour.

Press into an 11-inch tart pan.

Bake at 325 degrees F oven for 20 to 25 minutes or until golden brown.

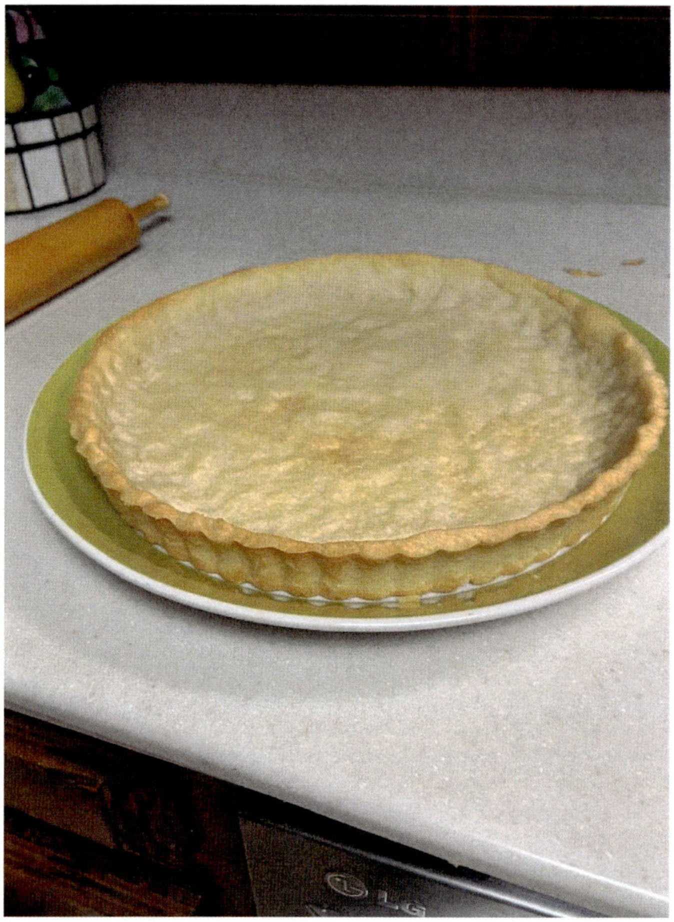

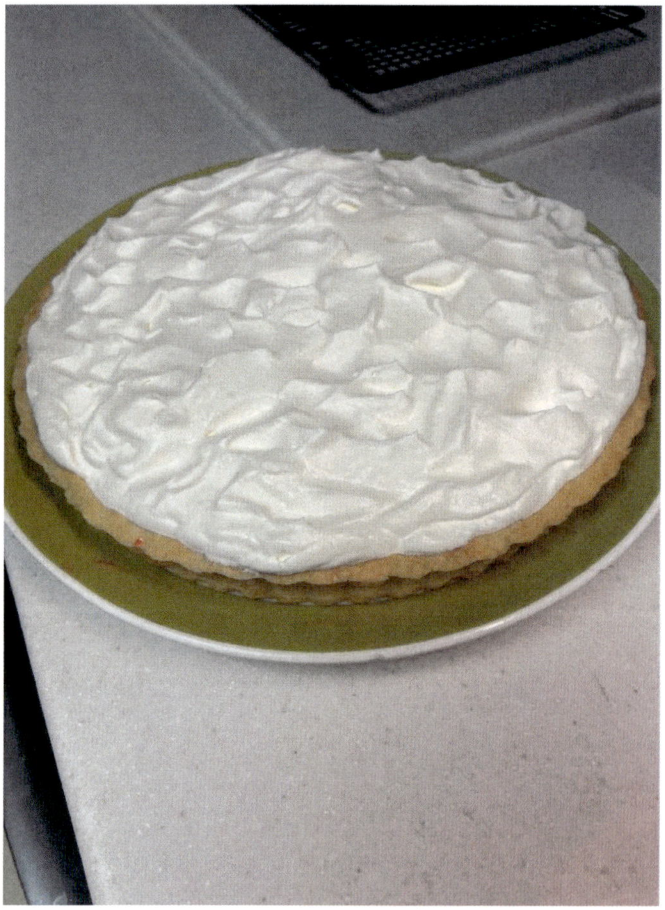

Grandma Spurgin's Chocolate Sheet Cake

Dave and Melba G. Tamplen

Top row: Charles, Dave (Junior), JW (Jack)
Bottom Row: Ralph, Davis Roy, Lexie, Harold Tamplen

INGREDIENTS

2 cups flour
2 cups sugar
½ teaspoon salt
2 sticks Oleo
1 cup water
3 tablespoons Cocoa
2 eggs, beaten
1 teaspoon baking soda
½ cup buttermilk
1 teaspoon vanilla

Frosting Ingredients:
1 stick Oleo
3 tablespoons Cocoa
6 tablespoons milk
1 box powdered sugar, sifted
½ cup chopped pecans
1 teaspoon vanilla

STEPS

Sift flour, sugar, and salt. In a saucepan bring Oleo, water, and cocoa to a boil. Pour over flour mixture. In another bowl, mix eggs, baking soda, buttermilk, and banilla together. Add to the first mixture and mix well. Flour and grease oblong cake pan Pour cake mixture into cake pan and bake for 20 to 30 minutes at 350 degrees F. Frost while hot as follows:

Mix Oleo, cocoa, and ilk in saucepan. Heat on low heat – DO NOT BOIL. Remove from heat and add the rest of the ingredients. Spread on cake while still warm.

    Makes 10 servings.

Grannie Jo's Fruit Cake

Terry and Joan Tamplin

INGREDIENTS

5 ounces self-rising flour
2 ounces plain flour
1 ounce corn flour
5 ounces soft margarine or butter
5 ounces caster sugar
4 eggs
3 ounces Glace cherries
8 ounces Sultanas
1 ounce ground almonds
1 ounce flaked almonds

STEPS

Grease and line seven inch round cake tin or square tin of equivalent size.

Wash cherries, dry, and cut in half.

Put sugar, fat, flour, and eggs in mixing bowl and blend together with electric mixer. Add almonds and sultanas. Mix with wooden spoon.

Put half of mixture into prepared tin, then make a layer with halved cherries, and then put the rest of the mixture on top. Sprinkle with flaked almonds.

Bake for 1 to 1 ½ hours in a moderate oven (160 Cicrotherm, 350 degrees F, Mark 5 gas) until well risen and golden brown. After the first 15 minutes lay some grease proof paper over the top of the cake to prevent it from getting too brown.

Leave on wire rack to cool, then turn out of tin.

Makes 6 servings.

Granny's Cap N Crunch Snacks

Dewayne and Kris Tamplen

INGREDIENTS

1 C sugar
1 C kayro syrup

Bring to boil in microwave

Add:
1 1/2 C. peanut butter
1 tsp vanilla
3 - 3 1/2 C Cap-N-Crunch cereal (plain)

Harold Tamplen

Granny's Chocolate Fudge Pie

Lexie Mae Tamplen as reconstructed by Brian Tamplen & Frankie A. Tamplen

This recipe was my favorite growing up. It's a simple recipe but was lost to my family after my grandmother passed away. My mother, Frankie A. Tamplen helped me to reconstruct this recipe. It's still one of my favorites! I remember sitting in my Granny's house as a kid with a cold glass of milk (from the cow that she had milked earlier!) while eating this pie! Great memories!

TRY DOUBLING THE RECIPE – IT'S THE BEST!

INGREDIENTS

2/3 cups sugar
2 ½ tablespoons Cocoa
3 tablespoons butter, room temp
2/3 cup light Karo syrup (try dark Karo syrup!)
2 tablespoons flour
1 teaspoon vanilla
2 eggs
1 dash salt
Frozen Pie Crust (use deep dish if doubling recipe)

STEPS

Mix sugar, salt, flour, and cocoa together. In separate bowl, mix syrup, vanilla, eggs, and butter. Combine bowls. Pour into pie crust. Bake at 375 degrees F for 45 minutes. Make sure crust does not burn (may have to place aluminum foil over edge of crust in last 20 minutes of cooking). If burning, turn temp down.

Taste great cold!

Makes 8 servings.

Harold, Brian, Dewayne, and Randy Tamplen

Ice Cream Dessert

Frankie A. Tamplen

INGREDIENTS

2 cups flour
2 sticks margarine (room temperature)
½ cup 3-minute Oats
½ cup brown sugar
1 ½ cups finely chopped pecans

STEPS

Mix and put on cookie sheet ¼-inch thick – smooth out even.

Bake at 25 to 30 minutes at 350 degrees.

Cool and crumble. Spread half of crumbs on bottom of 3-quart dish (9" x 13").

Spoon ½ gallon soft vanilla ice cream on crumbs.

Spread 1 jar Kraft Carmel topping over ice cream.

Add the rest of crumbs.

Freeze.

Key Lime Pie

Addie Ann Spicer Tamplen

INGREDIENTS

4 eggs, separated
8 ounces cream cheese
½ cup lime juice
1 14-ounce can sweetened condensed milk
½ teaspoon cream of tartar
1/3 cup sugar

STEPS

Beat egg yolks well, heat over low heat until color lightens and start to thicken. Mix in cream cheese carefully. Add lime juice and milk. Stir until thick. Pour into baked graham cracker pie shell.

For topping, beat egg whites, cream of tartar, and then gradually add sugar until peaks form. Spread on top of pie. Bake at 350 degrees F for 20 minutes.

Makes 8 servings.

Layered Pumpkin Pie

Ralph and Francille Tamplen

INGREDIENTS

1 graham cracker pie crust, 9-inch
4 ounces cream cheese – softened
1 tablespoon milk
1 tablespoon sugar
1 ½ cups Cool Whip
1 cup milk
2 4-ounce pack vanilla instant pudding
1 16-ounce can pumpkin
1 teaspoon ground cinnamon
½ teaspoon ground ginger
¼ teaspoon ground cloves

STEPS

Mix cream cheese, 1 tablespoon milk, and 1 tablespoon sugar in large bowl with wire whisk until smooth. Gently stir in Cool Whip. Spread on bottom of crust.

Beat 1 cup milk with pudding mix until well blended, 1 to 2 minutes (mixture will be thick).

Stir in pumpkin and spices using wire whisk; mix well.

Spread over cream cheese layer. Refrigerate for at least 3 hours.

Garnish with additional whipped topping and nuts.

Makes 8 servings.

Lemon Bars

Dewayne and Kris Tamplen

INGREDIENTS

Crust:
1 C flour
1/2 C softened butter
e1/4 C powdered sugar

Filling:
2 eggs
1 C white sugar
1/2 tsp baking powder
1/4 tsp salt
1/2 Tbsp lemon juice

STEPS

Preheat oven to 350. Use a 9x9x2 pan. Mix 1 cup flour and 1/2 cup softened butter and 1/4 cup of powdered sugar. Work these ingredients together and form the crust. Bake this for 15 min in the preheated oven. While this bakes, use a mixer to mix together 2 eggs, 1 cup white sugar, 1/2 tsp baking powder, 1/4 tsp salt and 2 Tbsp of lemon juice. Mix these with the mixer for about 3 minutes. It should get frothy looking. Then after the timer goes off for the crust, pour the well mixed lemon mixture into the hot crust and put it back in the oven for 15 min. Then take out and dust it with powdered sugar. Let cool.

Cut and serve it warm or cool.

Lemon Pie

Harold & Frankie A. Tamplen

Frankie, Tad, and Harold Tamplen

INGREDIENTS

1 ¼ cups sugar
2 ½ tablespoons cornstarch
½ cup water
2 egg yolks, beaten well
½ cup lemon juice
9-inch pie crust, baked

STEPS

Mix sugar, cornstarch, water, and egg yolks. In saucepan, heat 1 ½ cups of water until lukewarm. Add in mixed ingredients and stir until thick. Remove from heat and add lemon juice.

Allow to cool and pour into baked pie crust.

Davis Roy Tamplen

Marquise au Chocolat

Brian K. Tamplen

Brian, Dewayne, Harold, and Randy Tamplen

INGREDIENTS

Chocolate Sponge Cake
10 whole eggs
10 egg yolks
1 cup oil
¾ cup plus 2 tablespoons sugar
1 cup plus 3 tablespoons flour
½ cup cocoa
¼ cup cornstarch
½ teaspoon baking soda

Chocolate Cream Filling
5 ounces semisweet baking chocolate
6 tablespoons strong black coffee
7 egg yolks
1 cup sugar
1 ¼ cups butter, melted
¾ cup cocoa
2 cups heavy whipping cream
¼ cup powdered sugar

Grand Marnier Sauce
1 cup heavy whipping cream
1 cup sugar

Grated rind from 1 orange
1 cup orange juice
½ cup Grand Marnier
Few drops yellow food coloring

Assembly
4 cups strong black coffee
Grand Marnier Sauce

STEPS

Chocolate Sponge Cake
Sift dry ingredients together. Whip whole eggs, egg yolks, oil, and sugar in the top of a double boiler over low heat with a mixer at high speed until mixture is pale yellow and forms a ribbon. Remove from heat and slowly add dry ingredients. Pour batter into a well-buttered 10x15 inch cake pan and bake for 40 minutes at 325 degrees F. Remove from oven and cool in pan for 5 minutes. Remove cake from pan and allow to cool thoroughly on rack.

Chocolate Cream Filling
Stir the semisweet chocolate and coffee in a saucepan set over almost simmering water until chocolate is melted and smooth. Mix yolks and sugar together in a bowl, whipping until mixture becomes a glossy, pale yellow. Cool the chocolate and coffee and mix into the egg yolk mixture. In another bowl, mix the melted butter and cocoa then fold into the chocolate and egg yolk mixture. Whip the cream to soft peaks. Add the powdered sugar and whip to stiff peaks. Fold whipped cream carefully into the chocolate mixture. Reserve.

Grand Marnier Sauce
Combine all the ingredients in a bowl and mix well. Reserve.

Assembly.
Slice sponge cake into 1/2-inch thick strips and brush with the coffee. Line the bottom and sides of a 5x9 inch loaf pan with waxed paper cut to fit. Cover the bottom and sides of the pan with the strips of the cake. Spoon the chocolate cream filling over the cake strips. Cover the top with more coffee-soaked cake strips. Cover with aluminum foil and place a 1-pound weight on the top. Refrigerate overnight. Remove the aluminum foil and reverse dessert on a serving platter to unmold. To serve, pour the Grand Marnier sauce on the bottom of the servicing plates and place the sliced marquise on top.

Makes 8 servings.

Maw's Lemon Pie

Addie Ann Spicer Tamplen

INGREDIENTS

1 1/3 cups sugar
6 tablespoons cornstarch
1 ¼ cups boiling water
3 eggs, separated
1/3 cups lemon juice
2 tablespoons butter
2 teaspoons lemon rind
9-inch pie crust – baked
7 ounces marshmallow cream

STEPS

Combine sugar and cornstarch in pan – add boiling water. Bring to a boil, stirring constantly. Cook one minute or until mixture is clear. Stir in small amount of sugar. Mix into beaten egg yolks. Return to sugar mix. Cook over medium heat three minutes – stirring constantly. Stir in lemon juice, lemon rind, and butter. Pour into pie shell.

Beat egg whites until peak. Gradually add marshmallow. Beat until stiff peak. Spread over filling. Bake at 350 degrees F 12 – 15 minutes or until slightly browned.

Cool.

    Makes 6 servings.

Melba's Peanut Patties

Dave and Melba Tamplen

INGREDIENTS

2 ½ cups sugar, white
1 cup canned milk (Milnot)
2/3 cup white Karo syrup
3 cups raw shelled peanuts
1 tablespoon Oleo
1 teaspoon vanilla
Few drops red food coloring

STEPS

Mix all ingredients in large deep pan and bring to a boil and let cook over low fire for one hour, stirring occasionally to keep from scorching. Add oleo, vanilla, and red food coloring. Remove from heat and beat two or three minutes until creamy, then spread on greased cookie sheet. When dry or breakable, break into pieces and eat.

Sandra and Linda Tamplen

Melba's Pecan Pie

Dave and Melba Tamplen

INGREDIENTS

3 eggs
1 cup sugar
¾ cup white syrup
½ teaspoon salt
1 teaspoon vanilla
¼ cup melted oleo
1 cup broken pecans
1 9-inch unbaked pie shell

STEPS

Beat eggs well and add sugar, white syrup, salt, and vanilla. Mix well. Stir in melted oleo and broken pecans. Pour into unbaked 9-inch pie shell. Bake 45 to 55 minutes in 350 degrees F oven.

Bill. Lexie Mae, Ann Tamplen

Meringue

Harold and Frankie Tamplen

Randy Tamplen

INGREDIENTS

3 egg whites
6 tablespoons sugar
¼ teaspoon cream of tartar

STEPS

Beat egg whites and cream of tartar until foamy.

Beat in sugar one tablespoon at a time. Continue beating until stiff and glossy. Do not under beat. Heap meringue onto hot pie filling, spreading over filling carefully, sealing meringue to edge of crust to prevent shrinking and weeping.

Bake at 295 degrees F for 40 to 45 minutes or until golden brown.

Cool away from draft.

Makes 8 servings.

Microwave Peanut Brittle

Dewayne and Kris Tamplen

INGREDIENTS

1 cup raw peanuts
1 cup sugar
½ cup white corn syrup
1/8 teaspoon salt
1 tablespoon butter
1 teaspoon baking soda
1 teaspoon vanilla

STEPS

Stir together peanuts, sugar, syrup and salt in 1 1/2 qt casserole. (I use a Pyrex type clear measuring bowl with a handle).

Place in microwave oven and cook 7-8 minutes stirring well after 4 minutes. Add butter and blend well. Return to oven and cook 2-3 minutes more or until peanuts are golden brown. Add vanilla and baking soda QUICKLY and gently stir until light and foamy. Pour onto greased cookie sheet and let cool. Then, when cool, break into pieces and store in airtight container.

* with each microwave, I have to adjust my times. Sometimes I have to go on the lesser time end depending on the microwave.

Millionaire Candy

Harold and Frankie Tamplen

Randy, Harold, Dewayne, and Brian Tamplen

INGREDIENTS

2 pounds caramel candy – approximately 110 pieces
2 tablespoons evaporated milk
4 cups pecan halves
¾ pound chocolate almond bark

STEPS

Melt caramels and milk over double boiler (or microwave in glass dish). Pour in pecans and stir until coated. With buttered hands, drop on buttered cookie sheets in small patties. Let cool and dip in chocolate almond bark, Allow to dry on wax paper.

Makes 75 to 80 pieces.

Mimi's "Hard Sauce"

Dewayne and Kris Tamplen

INGREDIENTS

1/2 C butter
1 C powdered sugar
2 tsp vanilla

STEPS

Beat butter, softened, on high speed until fluffy and light (approx 5 min). Gradually beat in powdered sugar. Stir in vanilla.

Refrigerate 1 hour

(goes on pumpkin warm bread)

Tyler Tamplen

Mimi's Lemonade pie (makes 2)

Dewayne and Kris Tamplen

INGREDIENTS

1 12 ounce carton Cool Whip
1 can Eagle Brand Milk
1 6 ounce frozen lemonade
Yellow Food Coloring
2 graham cracker crusts

STEPS

Mix first 3 ingredients in order. Add a few drops of yellow food coloring. Pour 1/2 mixture in each crust. Refrigerate for a few hours before serving.

Oatmeal Chocolate Chip Cookies

Brian K. Tamplen

Brian and Addie Ann Spicer Tamplen

INGREDIENTS

1 ¼ cups butter, softened
¾ cups firmly packed brown sugar
½ cup granulated sugar
1 egg
1 teaspoon vanilla
1 ½ cups all purpose flour
1 teaspoon baking soda
1 teaspoon salt
3 cups Quaker Oats old fashioned uncooked oats
½ bag (6 ounces) semi-sweet chocolate chips

STEPS

Heat oven to 375 degrees F. Beat butter and sugars until fluffy. Beat in egg and vanilla. Add combined flour, baking soda, and salt. Mix well. Stir in oats. Stir in chocolate chips (optional). Drop by rounded tablespoons onto ungreased cookie sheet. Bake 8 – 9 minutes – careful not to overcook and burn cookies from the bottom. Cool and remove from cookie sheet. Store tightly covered.

Note some people like to add nuts (pecans, etc.). Feel free to make these your way!!

Makes 30 servings.

An interesting story behind this recipe. In the late 1980's I lived in Tyler, TX and this recipe was on the Quaker Oats box. I made these cookies often; however, around 1989 the company changed the recipe, and the new recipe was not nearly as good as the old one. But I had never saved the old recipe and I wanted that old recipe.

I decided I would go to every grocery store in Tyler to see if they had not sold out of the old boxes and buy it to preserve the old recipe. Not one had the old boxes with the original recipe. I was bummed for a bit. Suddenly a light bulb went off in my head. I would go to all of the convenience stores in and around Tyler to see if their inventory turn-over for Quaker Oats was much slower. I went to about 20 convenience stores without success; however, one day I was in Whitehouse Texas, a nearby community outside Tyler and went inside a small convenience store, and there it was – an old box of Quaker Oats that still had the old recipe. I immediately bought it and now have the cut-out side of the round box with this recipe.

Enjoy!

Old Time Apple Pie

Addie Ann Spicer Tamplen

INGREDIENTS

10-inch deep dish pie shell and top crust
6 green apples (or more)
1 cup sugar
1 tablespoon flour
1 dash salt
¼ teaspoon cinnamon
3/8 teaspoon nutmeg
1/8 teaspoon mace
2 tablespoons butter
1 tablespoon milk
2 tablespoons sugar

STEPS

Peel and dice apples. Arrange in pie shell. Mix sugar, flour, salt, cinnamon, nutmeg, and mace. Sprinkle over apples. Dot apples with butter. Put on top crust and crimp edges. Brush top crust with milk and sprinkle with sugar. Beat at 400 degrees F for about 40 minutes or until crust is brown.

Makes 8 servings.

Peanut Blossoms

Frankie A. Tamplen

Tad, Brian, Marci, Randy, Avery Ann, Dewayne, and Kris Tamplen

INGREDIENTS

1 ¾ cups flour
1 teaspoon baking soda
½ teaspoon salt
½ cup sugar
½ cup brown sugar
1 teaspoon vanilla
½ cup shortening
½ cup peanut butter (creamy)
1 egg
2 tablespoons milk
48 Hershey's chocolate kisses, unwrapped

STEPS

Combine all ingredients except for kisses in large mixing bowl. Mix on lowest speed until dough forms. Shape dough into small balls. Roll balls into white sugar and place on ungreased cookie sheet. Brian likes to make the balls about the size of a key lime. Bake at 375 degrees F for about 7 – 8 minutes. Pull out of the oven and top the cookie with a kiss. Press down firmly so cookie cracks with the pressure. Place back into oven for 2 more minutes.

    Makes 24 servings.

Pecan Balls

Frankie A. Tamplen

Frankie, Harold, and Brian Tamplen

INGREDIENTS

1 cup butter or margarine
½ cup sugar
2 cups chopped pecans
1 teaspoon vanilla
2 cups sifted flour
Confectioners' sugar

STEPS

Cream butter and sugar until fluffy; mix in pecans, vanilla, and flour. Shape into balls; place on ungreased cookie sheet. Bake at 325 degrees F for 20 minutes. Cool. Roll in confectioners' sugar.

Yields 2 dozen.

Pecan Divinity Rolls

Frankie A. Tamplen

Randy and Brian Tamplen

INGREDIENTS

Filling
2 ½ cups sugar
2/3 cup light Karo corn syrup
½ cup water
2 egg whites
½ teaspoon vanilla

Caramel covering
1 cup sugar
½ cup brown sugar
½ cup light Karo corn syrup
1 ½ cups Half and Half coffee cream
¼ cup margarine
1 quart pecans, chopped

STEPS

Cook sugar, syrup, and water until the syrup is hard when dropped in water (hard crack stage). Pour slowly over the two egg whites that have been beaten until stiff. Add vanilla. Continue beating until very stiff and cool enough to handle. Use a little margarine on hands and form into 5- to 6-inch rolls. Put on waxed paper and let cool before dipping in caramel mixture. I put my rolls in the refrigerator overnight before dipping in caramel.

Caramel mixture:
Cook caramel ingredients until it forms a firm ball when dropped in cold water. Cool slightly. While still quite warm, dip rolls of divinity into caramel and then roll in chopped pecans. Takes 1 quart chopped pecans.

Makes about 12 rolls.

Pecan Pie

Frankie A. Tamplen

INGREDIENTS

1 cup sugar
1 cup light Karo syrup
1 dash salt
½ teaspoon vanilla
2 tablespoons margarine, melted
3 eggs, beaten well
1 cup chopped pecans
1 tablespoon flour

Pie Crust – in a deep dish 9 ½ inch pie plate
1 ½ cups flour
½ cup Crisco
1/8 teaspoon salt
4 tablespoons cold water

STEPS

Pie Crust – in a deep dish 9 ½ inch pie plate
Mix flour, salt, and Crisco using a pastry blender until it looks like small peas. Then add water. Form into a ball and roll out onto a floured surface and lay into pie plate.

Pie ingredients:
Mix all ingredients and pour into unbaked pie shell. Bake in a 400 degrees F oven for 15 minutes. Reduce heat to 325 degrees F for 35 to 45 minutes.

Makes 8 servings.

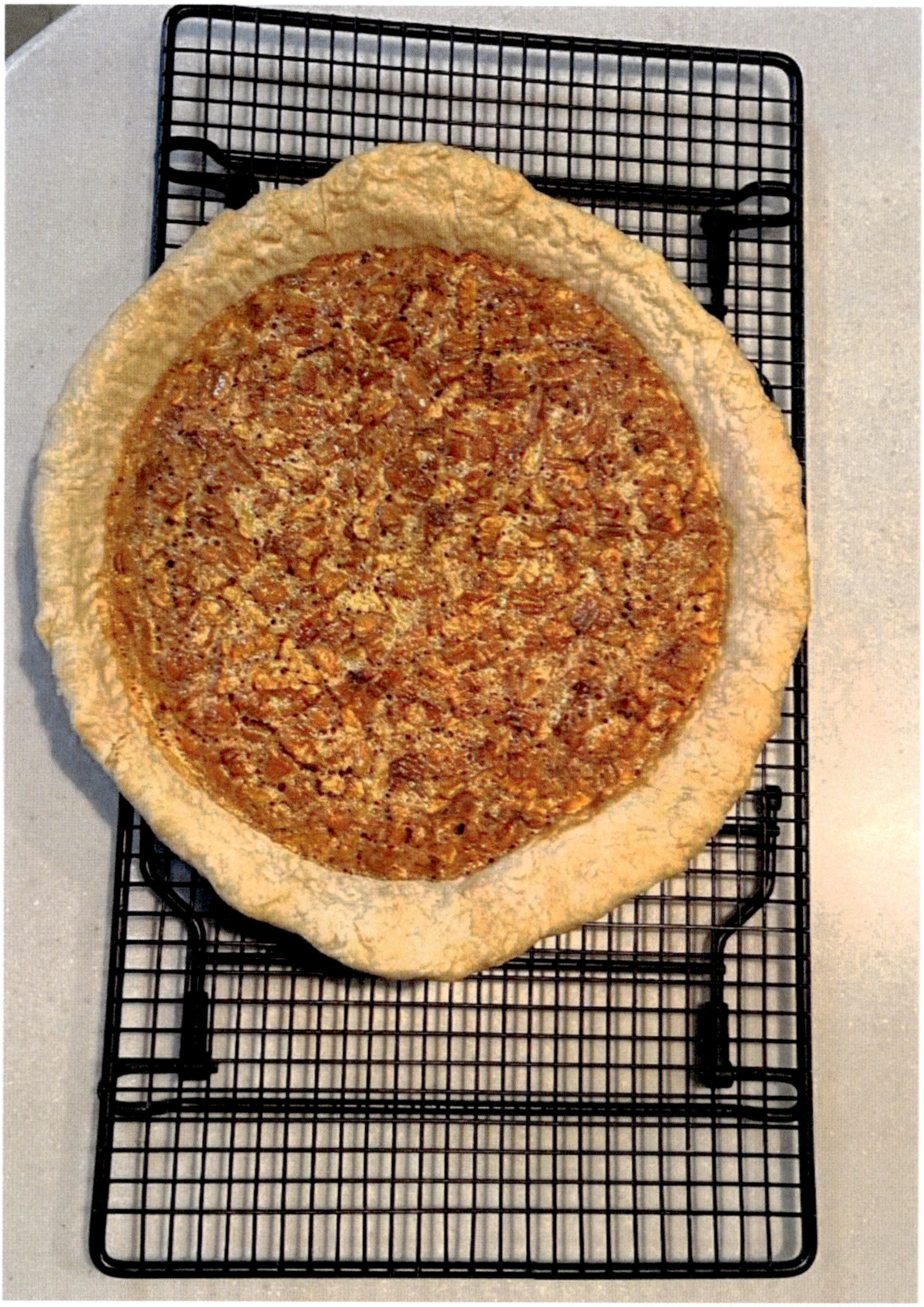

Pecan Tarts

Frankie A. Tamplen

INGREDIENTS

½ cup plus 1 Tablespoon Mazola margarine
½ cup sugar
2 egg yolks
¾ teaspoon almond extract
2 cups sifted flour

½ cup margarine
1/3 cup dark Karo syrup
1 cup Confectioners' sugar
1 cup pecans, chopped
Pecan halves

STEPS

Mix margarine and sugar. Stir in egg yolks, almond extract, and flour. Press evenly into tiny tart shells. Bake in 400 F degree oven 8 to 10 minutes.

Bring to boil margarine, Karo syrup, and confectioners' sugar. Stir in chopped pecans. Spoon intel shells. Top with pecan halves. Bake in 350 degree F oven 5 minutes.

Makes 24 servings.

Pineapple Coconut Chess Pie

Frankie A. Tamplen

INGREDIENTS

3 cups sugar
4 tablespoons flour or 2 tablespoons cornstarch
1 stick margarine (room temperature)
5 eggs, well beaten
1 teaspoon vanilla
20 ounces can crushed pineapple
1 small can Angel Flake coconut
Pinch of Salt

STEPS

In a large bowl, cream margarine, sugar, and eggs.

Add cornstarch, vanilla, salt, pineapple, and coconut. Mix well.

Pour into two 9-inch unbaked pie shells.

Bake at 325 degrees F oven for 50 to 55 minutes, or until knife comes out clean.

Polly Judd's Pumpkin Bread

Frankie A. Tamplen

INGREDIENTS

3 cups sugar
4 eggs
3 ½ cups flour
2 teaspoon baking soda
½ teaspoon cloves
1 teaspoon nutmeg
2/3 cup water
1 cup oil
16 ounces can pumpkin
1 teaspoon baking powder
¾ teaspoon salt
1 teaspoon cinnamon
1 teaspoon allspice

STEPS

Combine all ingredients.

Pour into three greased and floured loaf pans.

Bake at 350 degrees F oven for 1 hour.

Alternate: Can use 5 foil pans (7 ½ x 3 ¾ x 2 ¼) - fill each half full. Bake for 35 to 40 minutes.

Poppy Seed Cake

Frankie A. Tamplen

INGREDIENTS

1 Duncan Hines butter recipe golden cake mix
½ cup sugar
2 tablespoons Poppy seeds
4 eggs
¾ cup oil
1 cup sour cream

STEPS

Beat with mixer until all ingredients are well combined. Pour into a greased and sugared bundt pan. Bake at 350 degrees F for about 50 minutes or until toothpick comes out clean. Cool in pan for 5 minutes, then turn out onto serving platter.

Photo courtesy of Kolanowski Studios

Praline Cookies

Addie Ann Spicer Tamplen

INGREDIENTS

1 stick butter
1 egg, slightly beaten
1 cup flour
1 cup brown sugar
1 teaspoon vanilla
½ cup pecans

STEPS

Mix all ingredients and drop by teaspoonfuls on cookie sheet and bake at 325 degrees F for 20 minutes.

Davis Roy and Lexie Mae Tamplen

Prune Cake

Addie Ann Spicer Tamplen

INGREDIENTS

2 cups sugar
1 cup oil
3 eggs
1 cup buttermilk
1 teaspoon baking soda
2 cups flour
1 teaspoon nutmeg
1 teaspoon cinnamon
1 teaspoon cloves
1 teaspoon allspice
1 teaspoon salt
1 cup chopped prunes
1 cup chopped pecans

STEPS

Mix baking soda into buttermilk until dissolved. Mix remaining ingredients – in order – adding one egg at a time and beating well after each.

Bake at 300 degrees F for 1 ½ hours or until done.

Makes 16 servings.

Pumkin Bread

Dewayne and Kris Tamplen

INGREDIENTS

3 C sugar
1 C salad oil
4 eggs
3 1/2 C flour
2 tsp soda
1 1/2 tsp salt
1 tsp. nutmeg
1 tsp allspice
1 tsp cinnamon
2/3 C water
2/3 C canned pumpkin
1 C chopped pecans (optional)

STEPS

Mix together sugar, oil, and eggs. Sift together flour, soda, salt, nutmeg, cinnamon and allspice and add to sugar mixture. Then add water, pumpkin and nuts. Grease and flour 2 bread pans and fill each 1/2 full. Bake 1 hour 15 min. at 325. Cool on wire racks.

Mimi's "Hard Sauce"
1/2 C butter
1 C powdered sugar
2 tsp vanilla

Beat butter, softened, on high speed until fluffy and light (approx 5 min) Gradually beat in powdered sugar. Stir in vanilla. Refrigerate 1 hour
(goes on pumpkin warm bread)

Salty-Sweet Butter-Pecan Shortbread Cookies

Frankie A. Tamplen

Harold and Frankie A. Tamplen

Dewayne, Harold, and Brian Tamplen

INGREDIENTS

1 cup butter, softened (two sticks)
¾ cup unsifted powdered sugar
1 cup chopped toasted pecans
1 teaspoon vanilla extract
2 cups all-purpose flour
¼ teaspoon baking powder
1 cup turbinado or Demerara (raw) sugar
1 large egg, lightly beaten
42 pecan halves (about 1 cup)

STEPS

Beat butter in a stand mixer fitted with a paddle attachment on medium speed until creamy, about 1 minute. Gradually add powdered sugar, beating until mixture is smooth, about 1 minute. Stir in chopped toasted pecans and vanilla.

Whisk together flour and baking powder in a bowl. With mixer running on low speed, gradually add flour mixture to butter mixture until blended.

Transfer dough to a work surface; shape into two 7-inch logs. Wrap logs separately in plastic wrap; refrigerate at least 4 hours or up to 2 days. Remove from refrigerator 35 – 40 minutes before the egg wash.

Preheat oven to 350 degrees F. Line two baking sheets with parchment paper. Place turbinado sugar in a shallow dish. Unwrap logs, and brush evenly on all sides with egg. Roll each log in turbinado sugar. Cut logs into 1/3-inch-thick slices (you should have 42 cookies total), and place 1 inch apart on prepared baking sheets. Top each cookie with 1 pecan half, pressing lightly to adhere.

Bake in preheated oven until cookie edges are golden, 10 to 12 minutes. Let cool 5 minutes on baking sheets. Transfer cookies to a wire rack; cool 10 minutes.

Stuffed Pears Milanese

Addie Ann Spicer Tamplen

INGREDIENTS

6 large firm pears
3 ounces powdered sugar
4 maraschino cherries
¼ pound toasted almonds
¼ teaspoon almond extract
½ cup dry sherry

STEPS

Wash pears. Cut in half lengthwise and scoop out cores. Chop cherries very fine. Grind almonds until almost mealy. Add extract. Blend thoroughly all ingredients except sherry. Fill pear halves with mixture. Place in baking dish. Pour sherry over pears. Bake at 350 degrees F about 15 minutes or until pears are done but not too soft. Serve either hot or cold.

Makes 6 servings.

Sweet Pie Crust

Frankie A. Tamplen

INGREDIENTS

1/3 cup Crisco
1/3 cup plus 1 tablespoon margarine
1/3 cup powdered sugar
1 ½ cups flour

STEPS

Cream well Crisco and margarine. Add powdered sugar and mix well. Press into 9 ½ inch pie plate. Bake at 325 degrees F for 25 to 30 minutes or until golden brown.

Great with strawberry pie.

J.W. Tamplen

Sweet Potato Pie

Frankie A. Tamplen

INGREDIENTS

1 unbaked pastry pie crust – 10-inch
1 pound sweet potatoes (2 potatoes), baked in oven and peeled
¼ cup unsalted butter
1 can (14 ounces) sweetened condensed milk
1 teaspoon vanilla
1 teaspoon cinnamon
1 teaspoon allspice
¼ teaspoon salt
2 eggs, beaten

Praline Topping
½ cup Whipping Cream
1/3 cup firmly packed brown sugar
½ teaspoon vanilla
½ cup pecans, chopped

STEPS

Preheat oven to 350 degrees F. In a mixer, beat hot potatoes with butter (if you bake the potatoes the day before, just put them in the microwave to get them hot to melt the butter). Add milk, vanilla, spices, and salt; beat until smooth. Stir in eggs. Pour into pastry crust. Bake 50 to 55 minutes or until center is set. Cool. Top with the praline topping. You can keep it out on the counter until ready to serve and then if there is any left, you can refrigerate.

Topping
In small saucepan, combine cream, sugar, and vanilla. Cook and stir until sugar dissolves. Boil rapidly 5 to 8 minutes or until thickened, stirring occasionally. Remove from heat; stir in pecans. Pour praline on top of pie.

My pie cook time took between 45 and 50 minutes.

Teisen Carawe – Welsh Caraway Seed Cake for Afternoon Tea

John C. Tamplin

INGREDIENTS

1 tablespoon flour
2 teaspoons baking powder
5 ounces brown sugar
8 ounces butter
2 eggs
½ ounce caraway seeds
1 pinch mace or nutmeg

STEPS

Blend the butter into the flour and baking powder. Add sugar. Beat a little cold water with the eggs. Mix. Bake for 1 ½ hours at 350 degrees F.

Donnie, J.W., Dorthy, and Linda Tamplen

Winter Raspberries

Terry and Joan Tamplin

INGREDIENTS

2 packages raspberry Jell-O gelatin powder
Frozen raspberries, any amount
1 small carton double cream
1 small carton natural yogurt, Greek style

STEPS

Dissolve Jell-O in boiling water or as directed on packet.

Make up to 1 ½ pints with cold water.

When cold, but not set, stir in yogurt and cream. Then put in FROZEN raspberries.

Leave to set (the frozen raspberries speed the process of setting0.

Serve straight from the refrigerator, decorated with springs of mint (or as you wish).

Makes 6 servings.

ENTREES

Aunt Norma's Chicken 'n' Dumplings

Dewayne and Kris Tamplen

INGREDIENTS

3-4 chicken breasts
Lawry's seasoning
pepper
1/4 gallon milk
3 C Bisquick and 1 cup milk

STEPS

Boil breasts. Add a generous amount of Lawry's seasonings and peper as it boils. Cut up chicken and return to broth. Add approximately 1/4 gallon of milk. Return to boil. Add 1 cup milk to 3 cups Bisquick. Form into sticky dough and drop into chicken and broth. Continue cooking until dough is cooked and broth thickens.

Lexie Mae, David Jr, Davis Roy, Harold, and J.W. Tamplen

Autumn Stuffed Pork Chops

Addie Ann Spicer Tamplen

INGREDIENTS

¾ cup toasted raisin bread breadcrumbs
¼ cup diced unpeeled apple
¼ cup diced unpeeled pear
1 ½ tablespoons minced onion
1 tablespoon finely chopped celery
1 tablespoon butter (melted)
½ teaspoon sugar
¼ teaspoon salt
¼ teaspoon pepper
1 pinch ground sage
4 1 ¼ inch pork chops with pockets
1 tablespoon butter
2 tablespoons apple juice
1 tablespoon water

STEPS

Combine first ten ingredients. Stir well. Fill pockets of pork chops with stuffing mixture. Secure with wooden picks. Sprinkle chops with salt and pepper. Brown chops on both sides in 1 tablespoon of butter in a skillet. Add juice and water. Cover, reduce heat and simmer for 55 minutes or until chops are tender.

Makes 6 servings.

Baked Beans

Addie Ann Spicer Tamplen

INGREDIENTS

2 tall cans pork and beans
½ cup chopped celery
½ cup chopped onion
½ pound chopped bacon, cooked and crumbled

STEPS

Season with catsup, chili sauce, brown sugar, black pepper, salt, and chopped green pepper if desired. Add celery and onions to beans. Add seasoning. Sprinkle top with meat. Bake at 325 degrees F for 2 to 3 hours.

Randy Tamplen

Baked Cajun Chicken

Addie Ann Spicer Tamplen

INGREDIENTS

2 pounds chicken pieces
2 tablespoons skim milk
½ teaspoon dried thyme
¼ teaspoon white pepper
¼ teaspoon black pepper
Pam spray
½ teaspoon onion powder
¼ teaspoon garlic salt
¼ teaspoon red pepper

STEPS

Remove skin from chicken. Rinse and dry. Spray 13x9x2 inch baking dish with Pam. Arrange chicken meat side up if not boneless. Brush with milk. Mix other seasonings and then sprinkle over chicken. Bake at 375 degrees F for 45 to 50 minutes.

Brian Tamplen

Baked Cauliflower

Addie Ann Spicer Tamplen

INGREDIENTS

1 head cauliflower
2 tablespoons butter
2 tablespoons flour
1 cup milk
½ teaspoon salt
¼ teaspoon pepper
2 hard boiled eggs, chopped
2 tablespoons chopped pimentos
¾ cup chopped green onions
¼ cup buttered crumbs
2 teaspoons grated cheese

STEPS

Cook the whole cauliflower covered in 1-inch of boiling salted water – about 10 minutes. Remove from pan and cool. Melt butter, add flour, and stir in milk, cooking until smooth and thick. Add salt and pepper, eggs, pimento, and green onions to sauce. Place cauliflower in a greased baking dish. Pour sauce over cauliflower and sprinkle with crumbs and cheese. Bak at 375 degrees F for 10 minutes.

You might want to double the sauce amount.

Makes 6 servings.

Baked Corn Casserole

Addie Ann Spicer Tamplen

INGREDIENTS

1 egg
1 can creamed corn
1 bell pepper, chopped
2/3 cup milk
1 cup toasted bread
1 cup butter
1 onion, chopped
1 can whole corn
4 ounces pimento
1 teaspoon salt
1 teaspoon pepper
1 cup grated cheddar cheese
2 tablespoons sugar

STEPS

Mix all ingredients well and pour into greased casserole dish. Bake at 350 degrees F for 1 hour.

Makes 6 servings.

Baked Squash

Addie Ann Spicer Tamplen

INGREDIENTS

1 ½ pounds cooked yellow squash
4 grated raw carrots
2 onions, chopped fine
1 small jar pimentos
1 8-ounce sour cream
1 can crem of chicken soup
1 teaspoon salt, pepper, accent
1 small Pepperidge Farm cornbread dressing package
1 stick margarine

STEPS

Melt 1 stick margarine and mix with Pepperidge Farm dressing. Spread half of mixture in bottom of casserole dish. Pour in squash mixture and sprinkle remainder of crumbs. Bake 40 minutes at 350 degrees F (does best in a shallow casserole dish).

Makes 8 servings.

Barbecued Beef Brisket

Addie Ann Spicer Tamplen

INGREDIENTS

8 pounds lean boneless brisket
4 ounces bottled Liquid Smoke
Garlic salt to taste
Onion salt to taste
Celery salt to taste
Worcestershire sauce to taste
Salt and pepper to taste
14 ounces Heinz catsup
½ cup brown sugar
½ tablespoon salt
½ teaspoon dry mustard
3 cloves garlic
1 catsup bottle of water
¾ tablespoon Worcestershire sauce
1/8 teaspoon cayenne
¼ teaspoon pepper
¼ tablespoon Liquid Smoke
½ teaspoon vinegar
½ tablespoon BBQ sauce

STEPS

Place meat in long shallow pan. Cover with Liquid Smoke and sprinkle generously with garlic salt, onion salt, and celery salt. Refrigerate overnight. Sprinkle generously with Worcestershire sauce, salt, and pepper. Cover with foil and bake at 275 degrees F for 5 hours. Combine remaining ingredients to make barbecue sauce and simmer 30 – 40 minutes. Cover brisket with barbecue sauce and bake 1 hour. Cool before slicing.

Makes 10 servings.

Best Baked Cauliflower Mac and Cheese

Linda Tamplen Botts

INGREDIENTS

6 – 8 cups cauliflower, chopped into 1-inch pieces (I use 1 ½ heads of cauliflower)
2 tablespoons butter
3 tablespoons flour
2 cups whole milk
1 ½ teaspoon salt
¼ teaspoon cracked black pepper
½ teaspoon garlic powder
2 cups shredded sharp cheddar cheese, 8 ounces, see note

STEPS

Preheat oven to 375 degrees F.

Fill a microwave-safe bowl with 1-inch water. Add cauliflower to the bowl and microwave on high for 8 minutes. Drain and set cauliflower aside.

In a large saucepan, melt butter over medium heat. Stir in flour for about 3 minutes. Gradually whisk in the milk, a little at a time, until completely incorporated and mixture is thick and smooth.

Remove from heat, salt, pepper, stir in garlic powder, and shredded cheese until melted and completely incorporated and smooth.

Stir in cauliflower. Transfer to a 9x13 inch baking dish.

Bake for 25 minutes until cheese is bubbly and begins to brown. Switch oven to Broil for 2 – 4 minutes to brown the top a bit more.

Dish will be hot! Allow to cool slightly before serving.

Notes
For the cheese: DO NOT use pre-shredded cheese! I know it's tempting for the sake of convenience but please shred the cheese yourself. Pre-shredded cheese has a special coating to keep it from all clumping together in the package and this coating keeps it from melting properly in the sauce. It will end up grainy.

You can swap out some or all of the cheese for another kind. I have made this with white cheddar cheese and it is delicious. Try half white cheddar, half pepper jack for a bit of a kick!

Linda Tamplen Botts

Kaylyn Ann Botts and Tim St. Jean

Nick St. Jean

Logan St. Jean (right) *Troy and Brody Botts (on left)*

Broccoli Chicken

Brian Tamplen

Lexie Mae and Davis Roy Tamplen

INGREDIENTS

2 10-ounce frozen broccoli spears packages
2 sliced cooked chicken – 6 boneless breasts
2 cans cream of chicken soup
1 cup mayonnaise
½ teaspoon curry powder
½ cup breadcrumbs or croutons
1 teaspoon lemon juice
½ cup grated cheese

STEPS

Cook broccoli in salted water and drain. Arrange in baking dish. Place chicken (cooked) on top. Combine soup, mayonnaise, lemon juice, and curry powder and pour over chicken. Sprinkle top with cheese and cover with crumbs. Bake at 350 degrees F for 25 – 30 minutes.

Brian Tamplen

Cashew Chicken

Addie Ann Spicer Tamplen

INGREDIENTS

3 whole chicken breasts
½ pound snow peas or 2 packages frozen pods
½ pound mushrooms
4 green onions
1 15-ounce can bamboo shoots, drained
1 tablespoon chicken stock base dissolved in 1 cup water or 1 cup can broth
¼ cup soy sauce
2 tablespoons cornstarch
½ teaspoon sugar
½ teaspoon salt
¼ cup salad oil
1 4-ounce package cashew nuts

STEPS

Slice chicken in 1/8-inch-thick slices and then cut into 1-inch squares. Cut green part of onion in 1-inch length. Slice bamboo shoots. Mix together soy sauce, cornstarch, sugar, and salt. Pour in small pitcher. Heat 1 tablespoon of the oil at 350 degrees F and add nuts, cooking 1 minute more in pan. Add remaining oil and add chicken and cook. Add peas and mushrooms. Pour in broth, cover and simmer 2 minutes. Add bamboo shoots. Stir in soy sauce mixture and cook until thick, stirring constantly, then simmer 1 minute uncovered. Mix in green onions. Sprinkle with nuts.

Makes 8 servings.

Chicken and Dumplings

Brian K. Tamplen

INGREDIENTS

1 large whole chicken
2 cups flour
1/3 cup Crisco
4 tablespoons water

STEPS

Cook chicken in a slow cooker at high temp setting until done (meat falls from bone). Take chicken from bone and pour chicken and juice into a stove top pan.

Dough:
Take flour with a dash of salt. Add Crisco. Add water until doughy. Roll out very thin and cut into dumplings (use flour to keep from sticking to countertop).

Add touch of butter to chicken and juice and bring to boil. Drop dough into this mixture. Turn heat down until done.

Makes 8 servings.

Chicken and Spaghetti

Addie Ann Spicer Tamplen

INGREDIENTS

1 large chicken or boneless chicken pieces
Oil for browning
Chopped onion
Chopped bell pepper
Chopped mushrooms, optional
Chopped celery, optional
1 14-ounce bottle ketchup
1 12-ounce bottle chili sauce
1/3 cup red wine vinegar
1/3 cup brown sugar
Prepared mustard
Garlic clove, minced
Salt and pepper
Spaghetti

STEPS

Bake chicken in oil in skillet. Set aside. In same skillet sauté onion, green pepper, mushrooms, and celery. Add brown sugar, vinegar, mustard, ketchup, and chili sauce. Add 1 bottle of water (ketchup bottle) and 1 chili sauce bottle of water. More water may be needed. Add garlic, salt, and pepper. Simmer about an hour or more. Meanwhile place chicken on baking pan. Bake at 350 degrees F for about 1 hour basting with some of the sauce. Cook spaghetti and serve.

Makes 8 servings.

Chicken Enchiladas

Ralph and Francille Tamplen

Terilyn, Dewayne, Randy, Tani, and Brian Tamplen

Tani and Dorthy Tamplen

INGREDIENTS

2 cans chicken breasts, drained
½ cup chopped onion
2 10-ounce cans enchilada sauce
8 ounces shredded cheese
12 9-inch flour tortillas

STEPS

Preheat oven to 350 degrees.

Break apart chicken breasts with fork. Combine chicken, onion, 1 can enchilada sauce, and half of shredded cheese.

Fill tortillas with mixture, roll up, and place seam-side down in greased glass baking dish. Pour remaining enchilada sauce over top of filled tortillas, sprinkle with remaining cheese.

Bake for 15 to 20 minutes.

Serve with shredded lettuce and sour cream.

Chicken Kiev

Addie Ann Spicer Tamplen

Betty Ann and David Tamplen

INGREDIENTS

¼ cup plus 2 tablespoons butter, softened
1 tablespoon fresh parsley
1 small clove garlic, minced
¼ teaspoon dried whole tarragon
¼ teaspoon salt
1/8 teaspoon ground white pepper
6 chicken breast halves, skinned and boned
1 egg, beaten
1 tablespoon water
½ cup all purpose flour
2 cups soft bread crumbs
Vegetable oil

STEPS

Combine first six ingredients in bowl. Stir until blended well. Shape butter mixture into 3-inch sticks. Cover and freeze about 45 minutes. Place chicken breast halves between two sheets of wax paper. Flatten to ¼-inch thickness using mallet or roll pin. Cut butter stick into six pats, then place one pat in center of each chicken breast. Fold long sides of chicken over butter and then fold ends over. Secure with wooden picks.

Combine egg and water, beating well. Dredge each piece of chicken in flour. Dip in egg mixture and dredge in breadcrumbs. Fry chicken 4 or 5 minutes in oil or until done.

Drain well.

Makes 6 servings.

Chicken Pot Pie

Addie Ann Spicer Tamplen

Harold Tamplen

INGREDIENTS

3 tablespoons butter
1 ¼ cups chicken broth
2 cups cubed cooked onion
1 ½ teaspoons salt
1/8 teaspoon pepper
Flake pastry
¼ cup flour
1 cup milk
1 ½ cups peas and carrots, cooked
¼ teaspoon poultry seasoning
2 hardboiled eggs, sliced

STEPS

Melt butter in large heavy saucepan. Blend in flour. Cook low until thick, stirring constantly. Add chicken, peas, carrots, seasoning, eggs, chicken broth, and milk. Heat well. Spoon into 1 ½ quart casserole dish. Top with flakey pastry. Turn pastry edge under. Press firmly onto rim of dish. Cut slits for steam. Bake at 400 degrees F for 30 minutes or until golden brown. Optional: Add garlic powder and pimento in beginning.

Addie Ann Spicer Tamplen, Brian Tamplen, Avery Ann Tamplen

Chicken Squash Casserole

Dewayne and Kris Tamplen

Tyler and Krista Tamplen

INGREDIENTS

1 pound (2 cups) squash, cooked and drained
2 carrots, grated
1 onion
1 chicken, cooked and boned
1 can cream of chicken soup
1 package Pepperidge Farm stuffing (or Stove Top)
1 stick oleo
Salt
Pepper

STEPS

Melt oleo and pour over stuffing. Put ½ stuffing in a 9x13 inch pan. Mix other ingredients together and pour over stuffing. Pour the other half of the stuffing on top. This will freeze at this point. Bake (thaw if frozen) at 350 degrees F for 35 to 40 minutes. Cook until bubbling through.

Harold Tamplen

Cornbread Dressing

Addie Ann Spicer Tamplen

Brian and Addie Ann Spicer Tamplen

INGREDIENTS

2 boxes Jiffy cornbread
1 stick butter
½ cup chopped onion
1/3 cup chopped bell pepper
½ cup chopped celery
1 can beef consommé
Ground sage
Poultry seasoning
Salt and pepper
Chopped pimento

STEPS

Fix cornbread mix as directed (I sometimes use stone ground cornmeal and fix as directed). Crumble pieces and set aside.

In skillet, sauté the 1 stick of butter, onion, bell pepper, and celery.

Add cornbread to above mixture. Add sage, seasoning, salt, pepper, and pimento. Then add beef consommé. Put this mixture back into pan that cornbread was cooked and bake at 350 degrees F for about 45 minutes.

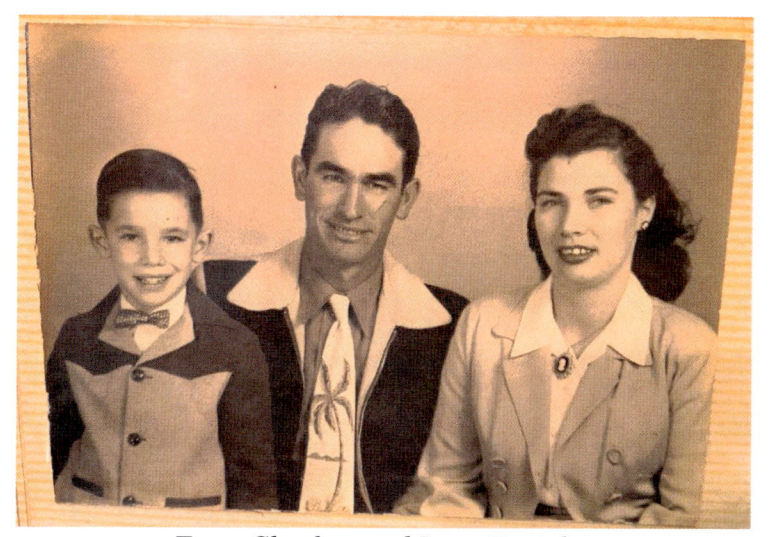

Troy, Charles, and Lena Tamplen

Creamy Chicken Rice Casserole

Addie Ann Spicer Tamplen

INGREDIENTS

1 cup wild rice
½ cup chopped onion
½ cup margarine
¼ cup flour
1 6-ounces can sliced mushrooms
Chicken broth
1 ½ cups milk
3 cups diced chicken, cooked
¼ cup diced pimento
2 tablespoons parsley
1 ½ teaspoon pepper
½ cup silvered almonds

STEPS

Prepare rice according to directions on package – I sometimes use one box of Uncle Ben's long grain rice and one box of Uncle Ben's wild rice.

Cook onion in margin until tender. Stir in flour. Drain mushrooms, reserving liquid. Add enough chicken broth to measure 1 ½ cups. Gradually stir in flour. Add milk. Cook and stir until it thickens. Add rice, mushrooms, chicken, pimento, parsley, salt, and pepper. Place in 2-quart casserole dish. Sprinkle with almonds. Bake at 350 degrees F for 25 to 30 minutes.

Makes 6 servings.

Daddy's Favorite Steak

Randy and Marci Tamplen

Randy and Marci Tamplen

INGREDIENTS

4 small steaks
Coarsely ground pepper
½ stick butter
¼ cup beef broth
2/3 cup heavy cream
½ teaspoon thyme
4 slices bacon, fried and crumbled

STEPS

Press lots of pepper into both sides of the steak. Heat skillet; add butter. When butter is melted, brown meat over medium heat. Remove steaks.

Turn heat to low and add beef broth to frying pan; stir well. Simmer for one minute.

Add cream and thyme and let simmer on low heat for a few minutes. Lasty, add crumbled bacon. Spoon sauce over steak and serve.

Makes 4 servings.

Davis Roy, Lexie Mae, and Maggie Tamplen

Dorito Delight

Frankie A. Tamplen

Harold and Frankie Tamplen

INGREDIENTS

1 package Doritos
1 pound hamburger meat
Salt and pepper to taste
1 can mushroom soup
1 can cream of chicken soup
1 small can condensed milk
1 can chopped green chilies
1 medium onion, chopped
Grated American cheese

STEPS

Spread 1 package Doritos in a 9x13 inch greased pan. Brown hamburger meat, medium onion, salt, and pepper. Drain liquid. Mix and add to meat 1 can mushroom soup, 1 can cream of chicken soup, 1 small can condensed milk, and 1 can chopped green chilies. Top with grated American cheese. Bake at 350 degrees F for 20 minutes.

Makes 5 servings.

Troy, Charles, and Lena Tamplen

Easy Chicken and Rice

Dewayne and Kris Tamplen

Dewayne and Krista Tamplen

Kris and Tyler Tamplen

INGREDIENTS

1/3 pound bacon, cooked and drained
4 large chicken breasts, uncooked
1 package Uncle Ben's rice
1 can golden mushroom soup

STEPS

Layer bacon slices on bottom of 9x13 inch pan. Pour Uncle Ben's rice (uncooked) over bacon. Do not add seasoning packet yet. Ay chicken breasts over rice. Spoon golden mushroom soup over chicken. Sprinkle seasoning packet from rice over soup. Pour approximately ¾ cup water around chicken. Cover and bake at 350 degrees F for about 1 hour. During last 10 minutes, remove foil and brown chicken.

Makes 5 servings.

Maggie and Andrew Jackson Tamplen

Filet Mignon Sicilian

Addie Ann Spicer Tamplen

INGREDIENTS

2 pounds filet mignon
1 medium onion, sliced
2 slices bacon
1/8 pound butter
½ cup marsala wine
Salt and pepper

STEPS

Have filets sliced to 1 ½ inches thick. Heat skillet – brown bacon slightly. Add onion and brown 2 minutes. Remove bacon and onion. Brown filet over high flame about 5 minutes on each side. Lower flame and continue frying 5 minutes, add salt and pepper to taste. Melt butter in separate pan and pour over filet. Add marsala wine and simmer for 2 minutes. Serve very hot.

Makes 4 servings.

Finger Lickin' Ribs

Dave and Melba Tamplen

INGREDIENTS

2 pound ribs

Sauce ingredients
2 tablespoons vinegar
1 tablespoon salt
½ teaspoon black pepper
¾ cup ketchup
2 onions, sliced
2 tablespoons Worcestershire sauce
1 teaspoon chili powder
¾ cup water

STEPS

Brown ribs and drain.

Add ribs and sauce ingredients into baking dish.

Bake uncovered for 1 ½ hours at 350 degrees F.

David, Jr Tamplen

Fresh Squash & Tomato Casserole

Frankie A. Tamplen

Frankie Ann Tamplen

INGREDIENTS

3 cups sliced yellow squash
½ cup green bell pepper
½ cup onion, chopped
1 large tomato, peeled and chunked (can use more)
6 tablespoons Bisquick
1 small jalapeno pepper
¾ teaspoon salt
½ cup grated cheddar or pepper jack cheese (pepper jack is best)

STEPS

Mix together in baking dish sprayed with Pam. Put cheese on top. Microwave covered for 5 minutes. Bake covered at 350 degrees F for 10 minutes. Remove lid and bake 10 minutes more.

Green Bean Casserole

Addie Ann Spicer Tamplen

INGREDIENTS

2 cans French cut green beans
1 can cream of mushroom soup
Cheddar cheese
1 can French fried onion rings

STEPS

Mix green beans and soup in casserole dish. Sprinkle with cheese. Bake at 350 degrees F for 15 minutes until hot. Remove from oven and place onion rings on top of casserole and return to oven for 5 minutes.

Makes 6 servings.

Grilled Chicken with Curry Yogurt Marinade

Addie Ann Spicer Tamplen

INGREDIENTS

½ cup plain yogurt
1 large garlic clove, minced
2 tablespoons chopped parsley
1 tablespoon lemon juice
½ teaspoon curry powder
¼ teaspoon ground cumin
¼ teaspoon salt
¼ teaspoon pepper
4 4-ounce boneless, skinless chicken breasts

STEPS

In a large bowl, stir garlic, yogurt, parsley, lemon juice, and then all other ingredients until evenly blended. Add chicken. Turn to coat with marinade. Cover. Refrigerate 3 hours. Arrange chicken on grill. Brush with remaining marinade. Grill over medium heat about seven minutes or until cooked throughout.

Makes 4 servings.

Grilled Reuben Sandwich

Addie Ann Spicer Tamplen

INGREDIENTS

2 cups sauerkraut, drained
¾ cup caraway seeds, optional
Thousand Island salad dressing
12 slices Rye bread (without carraway seeds)
6 slices Pumpernickel bread
12 slices Swiss cheese
2 pounds sliced Corned Beef
Butter

STEPS

Combine sauerkraut and caraway seeds. Spread Thousand Island dressing over 6 Rye/Pumpernickel bread slices. Arrange 1 cheese slice, 2 tablespoons sauerkraut, and 4 slices Corned Beef. Stack to make six 2-layered sandwiches. Spread remaining dressing on remaining Rye bread. Spread with butter and grill on toaster/griddle.

Makes 6 servings.

Hamburger and Bean

Sherrie Settle

INGREDIENTS

1 pound hamburger
1 can Pork and Beans
1/3 cup BBQ sauce
½ cup brown sugar

STEPS

Brown meat. Drain fat. Add other ingredients. Simmer 30 minutes.

Makes 4 servings.

Honey Lemon Chicken

Dewayne and Kris Tamplen

INGREDIENTS

1/3 cup honey
1/4 cup lemon juice
2 tsp rosemary leaves crushed
2 lb chicken

STEPS

Cut chicken into pieces and sauté. When chicken begins to turn white (not fully cooked), add other ingredients. Stir around until chicken begins to brown and other ingredients begin to thicken and caramelize.

Italian Chicken

Terilyn Tamplen

Donnie, Terilyn, Dewayne, Randy, Tani, Brian Tamplen

INGREDIENTS

6 boned and skinned chicken breast halves
Italian Breadcrumbs
16 ounces Ranch salad dressing

STEPS

Marinate chicken in dressing overnight or for several hours. Fold chicken in half keeping a generous amount of dressing in fold. Coat breast half with Italian breadcrumbs. Place on baking sheet (cover sheet with aluminum foil to aid clean up). Bake at 350 degrees F for 30 minutes.

Jack Tamplen

Meat Loaf Supreme

Addie Ann Spicer Tamplen

INGREDIENTS

1 ½ pounds ground beef
1 onion, chopped
½ green pepper, chopped
2 ribs celery, chopped
2 cloves garlic, crushed
1 teaspoon Italian herb seasoning
½ teaspoon oregano
½ package meat loaf mix
3 eggs
½ cup flour

Topping
2 tablespoons butter
½ cup chopped onion
2 ribs celery, chopped
¼ green onion, chopped
1 8-ounce can tomato sauce
2 tablespoons brown sugar
Worcestershire sauce, optional

STEPS

Combine all ingredients (except for topping) and place in lightly greased loaf pan.

Prepare topping – in saucepan, sauté onion, celery, and green pepper until soft. Add tomato sauce and sugar and simmer for a few minutes. Spread some on top of meat loaf and bake at 350 degrees F for about 1 ½ hours. I also add Worcestershire sauce to the topping mixture.

Makes 8 servings.

Mexican Corn Casserole

Addie Ann Spicer Tamplen

INGREDIENTS

¾ cup oil
¾ cup yellow cornmeal
1 teaspoon baking powder
½ teaspoon garlic salt
4 eggs
2 cans cream style corn
1 small can chopped green chilies
Salt and pepper

STEPS

Mix all ingredients well and bake in greased 9x13 inch dish at 350 degrees F for 45 minutes to 1 hour.

Makes 8 servings.

Mexican Cornbread

Frankie A. Tamplen

INGREDIENTS

1 ¼ cups yellow cornmeal
2 eggs, well beaten
1 cup milk
½ teaspoon baking soda
¼ teaspoon salt
1 can cream style yellow corn
¼ cup bacon drippings
1 pound ground hamburger
1 medium onion, chopped
4 canned jalapeno peppers, chopped
½ pound cheddar cheese, grated

STEPS

Mix cornmeal, eggs, milk, baking soda, salt, creamed corn, and bacon drippings together and set aside. Sauté meat and put on paper towel to drain. Grease a large iron skillet. Heat and sprinkle a very thin layer of cornmeal and let brown. Pour ½ the batter in skillet. Sprinkle meat, onion, peppers, and cheese on top and then pour the remaining batter on top. Bake at 350 degrees F for 55 to 60 minutes. Let cool 5 minutes and put on large plate.

Makes 8 servings.

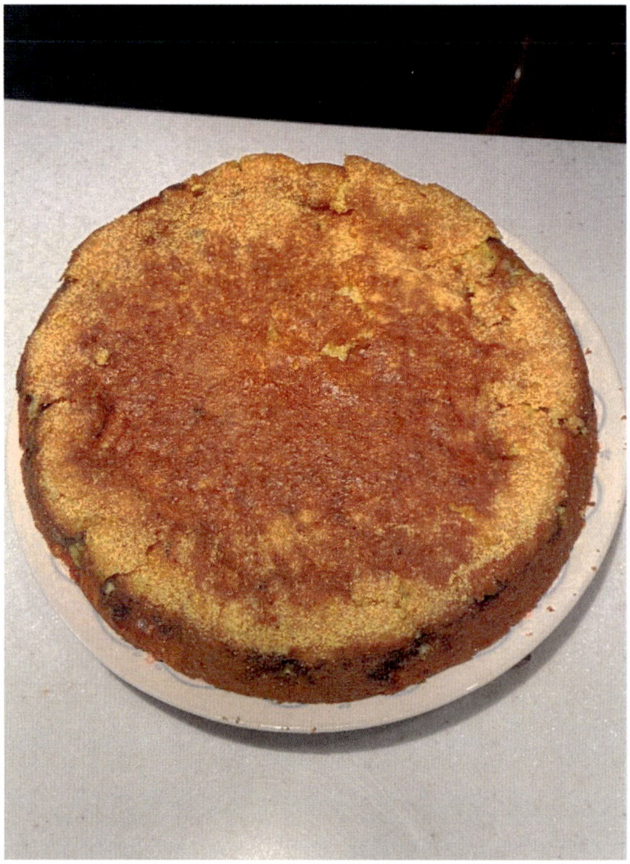

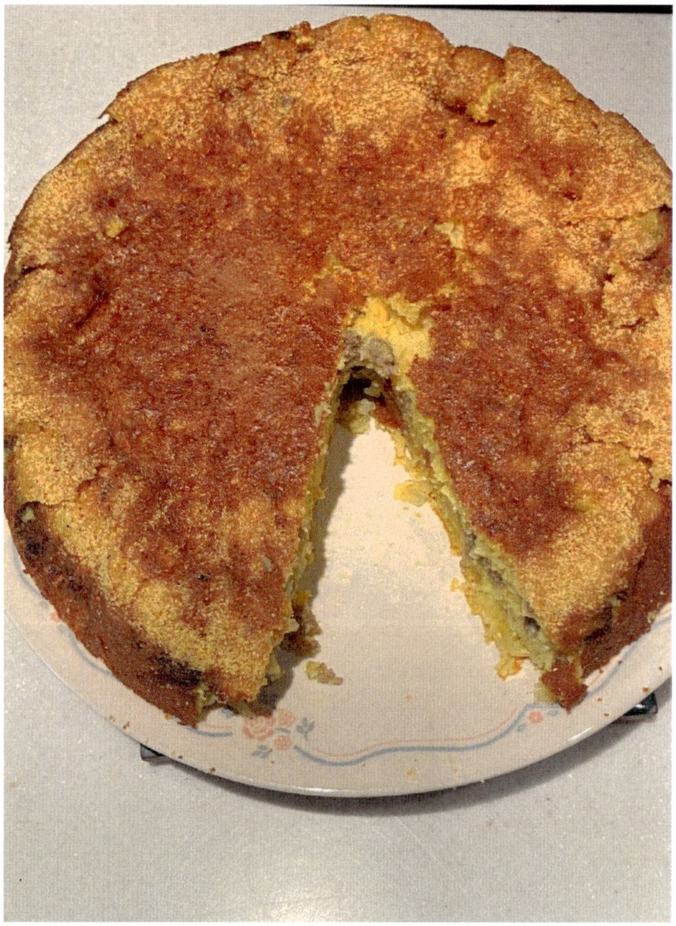

Mushrooms Parmesan

Addie Ann Spicer Tamplen

INGREDIENTS

1 ½ pounds mushrooms
2 tablespoons chopped parsley
2 cloves garlic, chopped
4 tablespoons grated Parmesan cheese
¼ cup olive oil
½ teaspoon oregano
¾ cups bread crumbs
Salt and pepper

STEPS

Clean mushrooms. Place in baking dish which has been brushed with 1 tablespoon olive oil. Sprinkle with parsley, garlic, oregano, half of breadcrumbs, and grated cheese. Add salt and pepper to taste. Pour balance of oil over this mixture, sprinkle with balance of breadcrumbs. Bake at 350 degrees F for 25 minutes. Add ¼ cup of hot water if mushrooms become too dry. Bake 5 minutes longer. Serve very hot.

Makes 6 servings.

One Dish Chicken and Rice Bake

Dave and Melba Tamplen

Charles, Dave (Junior), Ralph, Jack (J.W.), Harold Tamplen

INGREDIENTS

2 cans cream of mushroom soup
2 cups water
1 ½ cups uncooked rice
1 chopped onion
½ teaspoon paprika
½ teaspoon pepper
1 teaspoon salt
½ cup oleo
6 skinless boneless chicken breasts

STEPS

In 9x13 inch deep cake pan, melt oleo and then add soup, water, rice, paprika, salt, pepper, and onion. Mix well. Place chicken on rice mixture. Sprinkle with additional paprika and pepper. Cover. Bake at 375 degrees F for 45 minutes or until chicken is tender and rice is done.

Peppercorn Crusted Yellowfin Tuna

Addie Ann Spicer Tamplen

INGREDIENTS

6 tuna steaks (6 ounces each)
½ cup black pepper (cracked)
¼ cup Szechuan peppercorns
4 tablespoons allspice berries
4 tablespoons coriander seed
3 cups Cepe mushrooms, sliced
4 tablespoons olive oil
12 cups spinach, washed with stems removed
¼ cup shallots, minced
3 tablespoons garlic, minced
3 ounces Balsamic vinegar
Salt and pepper

STEPS

Toast peppercorns, allspice, and coriander in 350 degrees F oven for 15 minutes. Let cool Coarsely crack. Reserve. Dust each side of tuna in spice mixture. Heat 1 tablespoon olive oil until smoking. Sear tuna on all sides until lightly brown. Finish the tuna in 350 degrees F oven until done. In pan add 2 tablespoons olive oil. Add mushrooms. Caramelize until brown. Add spinach, shallots, and garlic. Sauté util spinach starts to wilt. Take the mushroom off and add to spinach when spinach is done. Place spinach mixture on middle of plate. Drizzle balsamic vinegar around spinach. Sprinkle with candied lemon zest and place tun on top of spinach/mushroom.

Variation:
Mix cilantro and olive oil. Marinate tuna steak. Add salt before sautéing. Sauté tuna four minutes each side on high heat (expect smoke from oil). Prepare mushrooms/spinach same as above. Dome onto middle of plate. Place orange vinaigrette around. Drizzle molasses over vinaigrette/spinach. Cut tuna steak and place on spinach.

Pork Tenderloin

Addie Ann Spicer Tamplen

Addie Ann Spicer Tamplen

INGREDIENTS

5 pounds pork tenderloin
Red wine
5 peppercorns or black pepper
1 bay leaf
5 whole cloves crushed garlic
½ cup flour
1 teaspoon salt
½ teaspoon dry mustard
1 teaspoon sage
1 tablespoon brown sugar

STEPS

Use glass baking dish. Marinate pork in first four ingredients for at least two hours. Turn once. Pat dry. Rub with garlic. Combine other ingredients and rub loin again. Roast in preheated 450 degrees F oven for 15 minutes. Pour marinade over loin. Bake at 350 degrees F oven for 1 hour.

Makes 10 servings.

Putanesca Pasta

Addie Ann Spicer Tamplen

INGREDIENTS

Olive Oil
8 cloves garlic, chopped
¾ cup green onion, chopped
Tabasco sauce (to taste)
5 dried red chili peppers
1 bunch cilantro (fresh)
1 can calamata olives – cut out pit and discard liquid
8 ounces chopped mushrooms
1 cup chopped parsley
1 large can peeled tomatoes
1 can anchovies

1 box Penne pasta

STEPS

Tan the garlic in olive oil on medium heat. Reduce heat to low. Add anchovies and allow to simmer, dissolving anchovies.

Add green onion, tabasco, chili peppers, Greek olives, mushrooms, parsley, and cilantro. Simmer 5 minutes or so. Add the tomatoes. Simmer 30 minutes. Cook Penne pasta el dente.

Add above mixture to pasta and serve hot.

Makes 6 servings.

Quail with Rice

Addie Ann Spicer Tamplen

INGREDIENTS

12 pieces game (quail or chicken)
Salt
¾ pound butter or margarine*
2 tablespoons cooking oil
1 large onion, chopped
2 medium garlic cloves, minced
1 can mushrooms
3 tablespoons flour
1 can beef consommé
1 can water (can from consommé)
¼ cup white or red wine
1 bay leaf
1 whole clove
2 teaspoons or cubes beef bouillon seasoning

STEPS

I have found that this much margarine is too much. I have reduced this amount by about half – you could probably use less than that.

Wash game, pat dry, and salt lightly. Place butter or margarine and oil in large skillet (the oil keeps butter from burning while cooking). Brown un-floured game (chicken). Lift out and place aide. In this skillet, add chopped onion, garlic, and mushrooms (retain liquid) and brown until golden in color. Add flour and stir. Then add consommé and can of water, wine, mushroom liquid, bay leaf, clove, and bouillon seasoning. Return meat to sauce, cover, and simmer for one hour or until tender.

Makes 8 servings.

Roast Peppered Rib Eye of Beef

Addie Ann Spicer Tamplen

INGREDIENTS

6 pounds rib eye beef roast, fat removed
½ cup coarsely cracked black pepper, can use less
1 tablespoon tomato paste
½ teaspoon garlic powder
1 teaspoon paprika
1 cup soy sauce
¾ cup red wine vinegar
1 tablespoon cornstarch (for gravy)

STEPS

Rub pepper over beef and press in with heel of hand. Place in shallow baking dish. Mix remaining ingredients and carefully pour over roast and marinate overnight. Remove marinade and bake roast at 325 degrees F for 17 – 20 minutes per pound for rare. Add 1 cup water to meat juices after baking for natural gravy or thicken this gravy with 1 tablespoon cornstarch mixed with ¼ cup cold water. I baste the roast with marinade and add a little water also.

Makes 6 servings.

Rosemary-Riesling Chicken

Addie Ann Spicer Tamplen

INGREDIENTS

8 chicken breast halves, skinned
Salt and pepper
2 tablespoons vegetable oil
¼ cup minced onion
2 cloves garlic, crushed
1 cup Riesling wine, or other white wine
1/3 cup canned diluted chicken broth
1 tablespoon minced fresh rosemary, or 1 teaspoon dried
1 cup whipping cream
Cooked rice

STEPS

Sprinkle chicken with salt and pepper. Brown chicken in oil over med/high heat. Remove chicken, saving drippings in skillet (non-stick). Place chicken in 9x13x2 inch baking dish. Add onion and garlic to drippings in skillet. Sauté util tender. Add wine. Cook over high heat, deglazing skillet by scraping particles that cling to the bottom. Reduce wine to ½ cup. Add broth. Stir well. Bring to just a boil. Pour over chicken in dish. Sprinkle with rosemary. Cover and bake at 350 degrees F for 20 to 30 minutes. Transfer juices and drippings in baking dish to skillet. Simmer. Reduce to ½ cup. Add cream. Cook over high heat stirring constantly four or five minutes until mixture thickens. Remove and pour sauce over chicken.

Serve with rice.

Makes 8 servings.

Salmon Lasagna

Addie Ann Spicer Tamplen

INGREDIENTS

16 Lasagna noodles
¼ pound shallots, coarsely chopped
2 tablespoons butter
8 ounces pernot drink – 1 part pernot, 3 parts water
6 tablespoons lime juice
16 ounces sour cream
3 bunches dill, coarsely chopped
1 teaspoon sugar
Salt and pepper
3 pounds fresh salmon
¾ pound gouda cheese (shredded)
1 small carton whipping cream

STEPS

Boil pasta 4 at a time in 4 quarts of water with salt and oil added. Place on flat surface to dry. Continue until all noodles are cooked. Save water. Sauté shallots in 1 tablespoon butter. Add ½ of pernot mix and ½ of lime juice. Add sour cream and cook until a thick sauce. Add dill and stir. Add sugar. Salt and pepper to taste. Intersect 2 noodles to firm a + sign. Add salmon to pasta water enough so skin can be removed. Cut salmon into 8 equal pieces. Spice salmon with salt and pepper and remaining lime. Place fish in center of pasta. Divide sauce into 8 sections. Place one on top of pasta. Overlap salmon with pasta. Place salmon into butter casserole dish. Butter brush squares. In saucepan take remaining pernot drink and cream. Bring to boil. Pour over noodles. Sprinkle gouda cheese over top. Bake at 400 degrees F for 15 to 20 minutes.

Makes 8 servings.

Saltimbocca Naples

Addie Ann Spicer Tamplen

Brian K. and Addie Ann Spicer Tamplen

INGREDIENTS

1 ½ pounds sirloin top or veal, sliced paper thin
½ cup flour
2/3 cup freshly grated Parmesan cheese
1 teaspoon salt
½ stick butter
2 tablespoons olive oil
½ pound thinly sliced prosciutto ham
½ cup finely chopped green onions
½ pound fresh mushrooms, sliced
½ cup beef bullion
2 tablespoons lemon juice
¼ cup marsala wine
1 ¼ pounds fresh spinach, stems removed
Salt to taste

STEPS

Step 1
Dredge sirloin slices in flour that has been mixed with 1/3 cup cheese and 1 teaspoon salt. In large skillet, melt ¼ stick butter. Add olive oil and brown sirloin on both sides, adding additional butter and oil if necessary. Drain the browned sirloin on paper towels. Quickly heat ham on both sides in same skillet. Place ham over sirloin.

Step 2
In the skillet used for browning sirloin, melt ¼ stick butter to begin making marsala sauce. With wooden spoon loosen bits from bottom of pan, add onions and mushrooms, sauté until tender. Slowly add bouillon and lemon juice. Cook until slightly thickened and add wine. If dry, add a proportionate mixture of wine, bouillon, and lemon juice.

Step 3
Cook spinach over high heat in the water that clings to the leaves after washing. When steam begins to rise from bottom of pan, lower heat and cover. Cook about 3 – 4 minutes or until spinach appears wilted and add salt. Arrange spinach on a large platter and cover with sirloin and ham. Pour remaining sauce over meats and sprinkle with remining cheese.

Sausage Zucchini Boats

Addie Ann Spicer Tamplen

INGREDIENTS

4 medium zucchini
½ pound sausage
¼ cup chopped onion
½ cup fine cracker crumbs
1 egg, slightly beaten
½ teaspoon MSG
¼ teaspoon salt
¼ teaspoon thyme
¼ teaspoon garlic salt
½ cup grated Parmesan cheese

STEPS

Boil whole zucchini 7 – 10 minutes or until barely tender. Cut lengthwise, scoop out cents and mash. Reserve shells. Brown sausage and onions in skillet. Drain. Stir in mashed squash and remining ingredients except the cheese. Stuff shells with mixture and top with cheese. Bake in a 9x13 inch pan at 350 degrees F for 25 – 30 minutes. This can be prepared and refrigerated before baking.

Makes 6 servings.

Spiced Cured Tenderloin with Dark Rum Glaze

Addie Ann Spicer Tamplen

INGREDIENTS

1 ½ teaspoons sugar
1 teaspoon course salt
1 teaspoon course ground pepper
½ teaspoon ground coriander
½ teaspoon ground allspice
24 ounces pork tenderloin
1 tablespoon olive oil
½ cup plus 1 tablespoon dark rum
6 tablespoons honey
6 tablespoons fresh orange juice

STEPS

Combine sugar, salt, pepper, coriander, and allspice. Rub spice mixture into tenderloin. Cover. Refrigerate overnight.

Heat oven to 375 degrees F. Tuck in the tenderloin ends to create a roast of even thickness. Tie with string if needed.

Place pork on rack in roasting pan. Brush with olive oil. Roast for 20 minutes.

Meanwhile in a small saucepan, heat the rum, honey, and orange juice until warm and well blended. Pour about 2/3 of the mixture into a small bowl. Set aside. Brush pork with remining 1/3. Return pork to oven. Roast tenderloin 25 more minutes, basting several times until meat is glazed. A meat thermometer inserted in the center should read 155 degrees F when done. Let stand at room temperature for 10 minutes before carving.

Slice the tenderloin across grain into ¼ inch slices. Serve with remaining mixture as a sauce.

Sunday Roast

Frankie A. Tamplen

INGREDIENTS

1 lean rump roast
Enough water to barely cover roast (Brian's comment: can substitute beef broth)
Light oil
Potatoes, peeled and cut
Carrots, cut

STEPS

Salt and pepper lean rump roast. Flour roast and brown with light oil in skillet. Put 1 ½ cups water in slow cooker and cook 10 hours on low heat. Add potatoes, carrots, and small onion. Turn heat to high and cook 4 more hours. Take up roast, leaving juice in pan.

Gravy
Take pint jar (16 ounces) and fill ½ full with water. Put 4 heaping tablespoons of flour into pint jar. Shake until smooth (mix with spoon if necessary). Pour into juice mixture in portions, heating until thick. Use enough mixture as necessary to thicken gravy. Serve hot.

Makes 6 servings.

Sweet and Sour Pork

Addie Ann Spicer Tamplen

Brian and Addie Ann Spicer Tamplen

INGREDIENTS

Sweet and Sour sauce marinade
3 pounds lean pork, cut into 1-inch cubes
1 cup water, cold
6 tablespoons cornstarch
Salad oil for deep frying
1 medium onion, cut into 1-inch chunks
2 thin carrots, sliced
1 cup sliced celery, about ¼ inch thick
1 1-inch piece ginger root, peeled and cut
1 thin cucumber, sliced 1/8 inch thick
1 green pepper, seeded and cut into 1-inch slices
1 can (5 ounces) bamboo shoots, drained
2 tablespoons sesame seed, lightly toasted

STEPS

Prepare sweet and sour sauce and marinade (see directions below). Place pork in pan with cold water. Cover and bring to a boil and simmer until tender or about 15 minutes. Drain. Pour marinade over cooled pork, marinate 30 minutes (stirring occasionally). Drain. Dredge pork in cornstarch. Heat oil in wok until hot. Fry a few pork cubes until crip and brown. Remove, drain on paper towels, and keep warm. Pour off all but 3 or 4 tablespoons oil from pan and reheat. Toss in onion, celery, carrots, and ginger. Stir-fry 1 minute. Add cucumbers and pepper. Fry 1 minute more. Add bamboo shoots, fry 1 more minute. Return meat to pan and pour in warm sweet and sour sauce. Stir until hot. Garnish with sesame seeds.

Sweet and Sour Sauce
Mix ½ cup brown sugar, 2 tablespoons cornstarch, ½ cup cider vinegar, 1 ½ cups pineapple juice, and 2 tablespoons soy sauce in saucepan. Cok over medium heat stirring until sauce thickens and becomes clear.

Marinade
Combine ½ cup soy sauce, 2 tablespoons sherry, 4 tablespoons sugar, ¼ teaspoon salt, 3 cloves garlic (minced) and a crushed 1-inch piece of fresh ginger root.

Makes 6 servings.

Sweet Potatoes with Pecan Topping

Addie Ann Spicer Tamplen

INGREDIENTS

3 pounds sweet potatoes, cooked and peeled
2 eggs
¾ cup light brown sugar, divided
1 stick butter, melted and divided
1 teaspoon salt
1 teaspoon cinnamon
1 cup fresh orange juice
1 cup pecan halves

STEPS

Mash potatoes. There should be about 6 cups. Beat in eggs, ½ cup brown sugar, and ½ of the butter. Add salt and cinnamon. Beat in enough orange juice to make potatoes moist and fluffy. Place in a 1 ½ to 2-quart casserole dish. Refrigerate if you wish. Just before baking, arrange pecans to cover top. Sprinkle with remaining brown sugar and drizzle with remaining butter. Bake at 375 degrees F for 20 minutes or until heated through.

I also add a little ground nutmeg. I chop the pecans and mix the remaining brown sugar, butter, and chopped pecans and put on top.

Makes 6 servings.

Tex-Mex Bean Burger

Addie Ann Spicer Tamplen

INGREDIENTS

1 ¾ cups cooked black beans, or 15-ounce can
2 tablespoons V-8 juice
¾ cup cooked rice
1 large garlic clove, minced
¾ teaspoon chili powder
½ teaspoon oregano
½ teaspoon salt
¼ teaspoon pepper

STEPS

Heat a lightly oiled grill. Rinse beans, drain. Dry. In a large bowl mash beans and add V-8, rice, garlic, and all ingredients until evenly blended. Shape into four ¾ inch patties. Mixture should be sticky. Damp hands should make shaping easier. Grill 3 minutes on each side or until brown and heated through.

Makes 4 servings.

The Famous Rice Dish

Randy and Marci Tamplen

Addie Ann, Tad, Brian, Marci, Randy, Avery Ann, Harold, and Frankie Tamplen

Photo courtesy of Kolanowski Studio

INGREDIENTS

1 can beef consume soup
1 can French onion soup
1 cup rice – not cooked
1 stick butter
1 can mushrooms (optional)

STEPS

Melt butter in a baking dish. When melted, add all other ingredients and stir. Bake for 45 minutes to 1 hour at 350 degrees F.

Makes 4 servings.

Welsh Leek Casserole

John C. Tamplin

INGREDIENTS

1 cup coarsely chopped leeks
2 tablespoons chopped parsley
2 tablespoons butter or margarine
8 ounces medium-wide noodles, cooked firm and drained
1 ½ cups creamy cottage cheese
¾ cup whole milk
3 large eggs
1 cup chopped cheddar cheese
1 teaspoon salt
¼ teaspoon pepper, preferably white pepper
¼ teaspoon caraway seeds

STEPS

Sauté the leeks in butter over medium heat for four minutes. In a large bowl combine cottage cheese, cheddar cheese, milk, and eggs. Beat until smooth. Add leeks, noodles, salt, pepper, and caraway seeds, and blend well. Pour into greased two-quart casserole dish. Bake in preheated 400 degrees F oven 30 minutes or until top is flecked with brown.

Makes 8 servings.

Wild Rice and Sausage Casserole

Addie Ann Spicer Tamplen

INGREDIENTS

1 pound sausage
1 pound mushrooms
2 medium-large onions
2 cups wild rice
¼ cup flour
½ cup cream
2 ½ cups chicken broth
1 teaspoon Accent seasoning mix
1 pinch thyme
1 pinch oregano
1 pinch marjoram
1 teaspoon salt
2 teaspoons pepper
½ cup slivered almonds

STEPS

Sauté sausage and drain on paper towels. Break into small pieces. Sauté mushrooms and chopped onions in sausage fat. Add to cooked sausage. Cook washed wild rice in boiling salted water for 10 – 12 minutes. Drain. Mix flour with cream until smooth. Add chicken broth and cook until it thickens. Season with Accent, oregano, thyme, marjoram, salt, and pepper. Combine with rice, sausage, and vegetables. Mix and toss together. Bake in a casserole dish for 25 – 30 minutes at 350 degrees F until it bubbles. Sprinkle with slivered almonds around the rim.

Makes 8 servings.

Wild Rice Curry

Addie Ann Spicer Tamplen

INGREDIENTS

¾ cup wild rice
6 slices bacon, diced
½ cup chopped onion
½ cup raw grated carrots
2 egg yolks
1 cup light cream
1 ½ teaspoons curry powder
½ teaspoon salt
4 tablespoons butter

STEPS

Cook wild rice until done. Drain and wash in cold water. Fry bacon then add onions and carrots. Sauté until onions are soft. Strain out and ix with wild rice. Place in buttered casserole dish. Beat in the egg yolks, add the cream and seasonings, and pour over the mixture. Dot with the butter and bake at 300 degrees F in a pan of water until set.

Makes 6 servings.

Wonderful Potatoes

Addie Ann Spicer Tamplen

INGREDIENTS

6 potatoes, sliced ¼" thick
1 package onion soup mix
Salt and pepper
1 stick butter
1 can chicken broth

STEPS

Mix all ingredients and bake at 350 degrees F for 1 hour.

Makes 6 servings.

Yellow Squash Casserole

Frankie A. Tamplen

INGREDIENTS

1 package Gladiola Yellow Cornbread Mix (baked)

Crumble baked cornbread and add 2 cups milk, 1 cup grated mild Cheddar Cheese, 1 can Cream of Chicken or Mushroom soup.

1 small or medium onion, chopped
1 tablespoon sage

Salt & Pepper to taste

1 quart yellow quash sliced, cooked, and drained

STEPS

Put in casserole dish and bake at 350 degrees F in oven until cheese melts (*I had to turn my oven up to 375 degrees F to get it to thicken*).

Top with more cheese (optional).

SALADS

Broccoli and Grape Salad

Frankie A. Tamplen

Frankie Ann, Brian, and Harold Tamplen

INGREDIENTS

1 bunch broccoli
1 pound bacon – fried (I used 7 or 8 slices)
1 cup seedless red grapes, cut in half (I use 2 cups)
½ cup red onion – sliced into rings
½ cup sugar
2 tablespoons red wine vinegar

STEPS

Mix broccoli, grapes, and onion together.

Put ½ cup sugar and 2 tablespoons red wine vinegar in small pan and bring to a boil. Boil for one minute. Let cool for about 10 minutes and add 1 cup Hellmann's Mayonnaise. Pour over salad.

Crumble bacon and add to salad just before serving.

Cwm Rhudd (Welsh red cabbage salad)

John C. Tamplin

INGREDIENTS

1 head red cabbage
1 cup white vinegar
1 cup sugar
1 teaspoon fennel seeds
½ teaspoon allspice
½ teaspoon ginger
½ teaspoon mace or nutmeg
Tiny dash of cinnamon

STEPS

Chop the cabbage slightly more coarse than for coleslaw and place in a large bowl. In a saucepan combine all of the other ingredients, bring to a boil and simmer for 20 minutes. Pour marinade over cabbage, cover, and let stand, stirring occasionally. When cool, cover and chill. Keeps well in the refrigerator. Serve as a salad or as a relish with meaty dishes.

Makes 4 servings.

Grilled Red Potato Salad with Warm Bacon Vinaigrette

Randy and Marci Tamplen

Tad Tamplen

INGREDIENTS

10 pounds new potatoes, scrubbed
3 tablespoons salt
1 ¼ pounds bacon
2 large red onions, sliced very thin
½ cup olive oil
¼ cup plus 2 tablespoons apple cider vinegar
1 cup light brown sugar
¾ teaspoon freshly ground pepper

STEPS

Add potatoes to a large pot of cold water. Bring to a boil; boil potatoes until almost fork tender. Drain.

Cook bacon in skillet until crisp, about 5 minutes. Remove bacon, crumble, and set aside.

Pour off all but 2 tablespoons fat.

Return skillet to heat; add onions and cook until soft, 3 to 5 minutes. Add 5 tablespoons oil, vinegar, and sugar; cook, stirring until sugar dissolves, 3 to 5 minutes. Add 1 ½ teaspoons salt and ¼ teaspoon pepper. Heat grill or skillet to medium hot. Slice potatoes in halve; toss with remaining 3 tablespoons oil, 1 ½ teaspoon salt, and ½ teaspoon pepper. Grill potatoes until crisp and cooked through, 3 to 4 minutes per side. Return potatoes to bowl. Add dressing and bacon, toss. Serve warm or at room temperature.

Makes 14 servings.

Mandarin – Pistachio Salad

Tani Tamplen Cook

INGREDIENTS

1 can crushed pineapple in juice
1 can Mandarin orange segments – use ½ of juice
2 small boxes pistachio instant pudding
½ cup pecans (optional)
1 cup miniature marshmallows
1 large Cool Whip

STEPS

Combine all ingredients and chill. Can be used as a salad or as a light dessert.

Makes 5 servings.

Francille and Ralph Tamplen

Mud Salad Dressing

Brian Tamplen and Addie Ann Spicer Tamplen

Lexie Mae Tamplen and Mike Highland

INGREDIENTS

3 pinches Herbes de Provence (from Williams Sonoma)
7 tablespoons balsamic vinegar
5 tablespoons extra virgin olive oil
2 ½ teaspoons Grey Poupon (or spicy brown mustard)
½ teaspoon sugar
3 cloves fresh garlic, peeled, garlic press

STEPS

Mix all ingredients well using heaping teaspoon/tablespoon for all ingredients and large pinches with herbes.

Makes 24 servings.

Lexie Mae Tamplen and Sandra Tamplen Highland

Vegetable Relish Salad

Dewayne and Kris Tamplen

Georges Tenie, Krista Tamplen, Addie Ann, and Brian Tamplen

INGREDIENTS

1 cup sugar
½ cup oil
½ teaspoon garlic
1 teaspoon salt
1 teaspoon pepper
Celery, chopped
Onion
Bell pepper
Pimento
Corn
Green beans, French style
Water chestnuts
Peas
Mushrooms

STEPS

Mix sugar, oil, vinegar, garlic, salt, and pepper together and add chopped celery, onion, bell pepper, pimentos, corn, french style green beans, water chestnuts, peas, and mushrooms. (This can be varied to add to any canned vegetables that your family enjoys).

Makes 5 servings.

Corbin, Bailey, Tyler Tamplen

SOUPS

Addie Ann's Broccoli Soup

Addie Ann Spicer Tamplen

INGREDIENTS

2 10-ounce packages frozen chopped broccoli
2 cans cream of mushroom soup
2 soup cans of milk
½ cup dry white wine
4 tablespoons butter
½ teaspoon dried tarragon (crushed)
1 dash white pepper

STEPS

In large saucepan, cook broccoli according to package directions. Drain. Add soup, milk, wine, butter, tarragon, and pepper. Heat throughout.

Makes 6 servings.

Addie's Homemade Potato Soup

Addie Ann Spicer Tamplen

INGREDIENTS

8 slices bacon
1 large onion, chopped
6 medium potatoes, cubed
2 10 ¼ ounces cream of chicken soup
2 soup cans of milk
Salt and pepper
Parsley flakes

STEPS

Cook bacon until crisp. Save 3 teaspoons of bacon drippings for sauteing onions. Add potatoes. Cover with water and cook until tender. Add chicken soup, milk, salt, pepper, and parsley flakes. Heat but do not boil. Serve with bacon on top.

Makes 6 servings.

Beef Vegetable Soup

Brian and Addie Ann Spicer Tamplen

Lexie Mae Tamplen

INGREDIENTS

1 ½ pounds lean beef cubes
4 large carrots, peeled and sliced in round discs
8 small to medium potatoes, peeled and cubed
1 can peas
1 can green beans
1 can whole kernel corn
2 tablespoons Worcestershire sauce
2 cups water, warm
2 cubes beef bullion
1 can beef consommé
8 pods okra (optional), cut
1 large can diced tomatoes
1 medium white onion, chopped
2 tablespoons garlic, micned

STEPS

Add beef cubes to stockpot and heat under medium heat.

As meat begins to turn brown, add Worcestershire sauce, beef consommé, and garlic.

Add beef bouillon to warm water and stir until dissolved. Add water and beef bouillon to stock pot.

Add all other ingredients to stock pot and simmer for 2 hours over low heat.

Makes 6 servings.

Brian's favorite Split Pea Soup

Addie Ann Spicer Tamplen

Brian K. Tamplen

INGREDIENTS

8 cups water
1 pound dried split peas (about 2 ¼ cups)
2 pounds smoked ham
1 medium onion, chopped
1 teaspoon salt
¼ teaspoon pepper
3 medium carrots, cut
2 medium celery stalks, cut

STEPS

Heat water and peas to boiling in Dutch oven. Boil 2 minutes. Remove from heat. Cover and let stand 1 hour.

Str ham, onion, salt, and pepper into peas. Heat to boiling, reduce heat. Cover and simmer until peas are tender, about 1 hour. Skim fat (if necessary).

Remove ham from peas, trim fat and bone from ham. Cut ham into ½ inch pieces. Stir ham, carrots, and celery into soup. Heat to boiling, reduce heat. Cover and simmer until vegetables are tender, about 45 minutes.

Makes 8 servings.

Chicken Gumbo

Addie Ann Spicer Tamplen

INGREDIENTS

1 medium onion
½ green pepper
3 cloves garlic
1 stalk celery
½ cup vegetable oil
½ cup flour
2 cups chicken stock
½ can Ro-Tel tomatoes
1 pound sausage
2 pounds chicken
1 package okra
Cajun seasoning to taste

STEPS

Chop onion, green pepper, garlic, and celery.

Combine oil and flour. Heat on medium heat until dark brown. Add chopped vegetables and cook until onions are clear. Stir occasionally.

Combine chicken stock and Ro-Tel tomatoes. Heat then simmer. Add roux with Cajun seasoning.

Brown sausage and chicken. Add sausage and chicken to mixture. Bring to a boil. Simmer until chicken is done. Sauté okra in butter with 1 cap full vinegar. Add to gumbo and cook 15 – 20 minutes before serving.

Serve over white rice.

Makes 10 servings.

Creamy Tortellini Soup

Dewayne and Kris Tamplen

INGREDIENTS

1 Tbsp olive oil
1 Tbsp butter
1 onion, diced
2 cloves garlic minced
pinch crushed red pepper flakes to taste
1/4 cup all purpose flour
3 cups vegetable broth
14.5 oz can diced tomatoes
8 oz tomato sauce
1/2 tsp dried basil
1 tsp Italian Seasoning
salt and freshly ground black pepper to taste

8 oz cheese tortellini (the refrigerated kind)
½ C freshly grated parmesan cheese
1 ½ cups fresh spinach leaves (packed)
½ cup heavy cream or half and half
¼ cup fresh basil leaves (chopped)

STEPS

Add oil and butter to a lg saucepan over medium heat. Once melted, add the onion and cook, stirring occasionally, 5 min. Add the garlic. Stir in the flour and cook for another minute.

Add the vegetable broth, diced tomatoes, tomato sauce, Italian seasoning, and dried basil. Season with salt and pepper. Taste broth and adjust seasonings if needed.

Bring mixture to a gentle boil and then add the tortellini. Cook for a few minutes, until tortellini are tender.

Remove from heat and stir in spinach, parmesan cheese, and cream. Add chopped basil. Serve warm.

Curry Mushroom Soup

Addie Ann Spicer Tamplen

INGREDIENTS

¾ cup butter
4 cups sliced fresh mushrooms
1 cup finely chopped onion
1/3 cup flour
3 tablespoons curry powder
2 teaspoons garlic powder
2 teaspoons salt
½ teaspoon pepper
4 cups milk
2 cups cream
10 ounces spinach – frozen, thawed, chopped, and drained
6 slices bacon, cooked and crumbled

STEPS

In large skillet melt ¼ cupof the butter. Add mushrooms and onion. Cook until tender. Remove from heat. In Dutch oven, melt remaining ½ cup of butter. Stir in flour, curry powder, garlic powder, salt, and pepper. Cook 2 minutes, whisking constantly. Gradually add milk and cream. Cook until thick. Sitr in mushroom mixture and spinach. Cook until heated throughout.

Makes 8 servings.

Five Hour Stew

Randy and Marci Tamplen

Avery Ann and Tad Tamplen

INGREDIENTS

2 pounds beef stew meat
1 medium onion, chopped
1 cup celery, chopped
6 carrots, chopped
2 cups tomato juice
1 slice bread, broken up
3 tablespoons Tapioca
1 tablespoon honey
1 ½ teaspoons garlic powder
½ teaspoon pepper
4 potatoes, quartered

STEPS

Mix all ingredients together and bake in a covered dish for 5 hours at 250 degrees.

Makes 6 servings.

Inn at Brushy Creek Portuguese Soup

Randy and Marci Tamplen

Randy, Avery Ann, Tad, and Marci Tamplen

INGREDIENTS

2 cups chopped onion
6 cloves garlic, chopped
6 tablespoons oil
2 pounds Eckrich Smoked Sausage
10 cups beef stock
1 can kidney beans
1 head green cabbage, cored and chopped
12 small new potatoes, scrubbed and quartered
½ cup vinegar
2 cups Ketchup
Salt and pepper to taste

STEPS

Sauté onions and garlic in oil

When vegetables are transparent add sausage slices and brown lightly.

Add remining ingredients.

Bring to a boil.

Reduce heat. Simmer 45 minutes to an hour.

Correct seasons to taste.

We usually half this recipe.

    Makes 8 servings.

Mexican Corn Soup

Addie Ann Spicer Tamplen

INGREDIENTS

4 cups fresh corn kernels
¼ cup chopped onion
2 tablespoons butter
2 tablespoons flour
Salt and pepper
2 cups chicken broth
2 cups milk or cream
1 cup grated cheddar cheese
¼ ounce can chopped green chilies
Tortilla chips
½ cup crisp bacon, crumbled

STEPS

Sauté corn and onion in butter until tender Add flour, salt, and pepper. Cook one minute. Gradually add broth, alternating with milk or cream until thickened. Add cheddar cheese and green chilies. Do not overheat. Serve in bowls with tortilla chips and bacon sprinkled on top.

Makes 6 servings.

Potato Cheese Soup

Dewayne and Kris Tamplen

Tyler, Bailey, Addie Ann Spicer

INGREDIENTS

8 medium potatoes
1 pound Velvetta
2 cups sour cream
¼ cup butter
Green onion
Bacon bits

STEPS

Boil potatoes in 4 cups water with 2 chicken bouillon cubes. Be careful not to boil the potatoes too soft! Add 1 pound Velvetta, 2 cups sour cream and ¼ cup butter. Add green onions and bacon bits on top when served.
    Makes 6 servings.

Santa Fe Soup

Dewayne and Kris Tamplen

INGREDIENTS

1 lb chicken (or ground beef)
1 lb Velveeta cheese
1 can stewed tomatoes
1 can corn
1 can Rotel
1 can black beans
1/2 chopped onion

STEPS

Brown chicken (cubed) (or ground beef if using) with onion. Add all other ingredients. Cook slowly so cheese doesn't burn. Simmer 15 min.

Santa Fe Stew

Frankie A. Tamplen

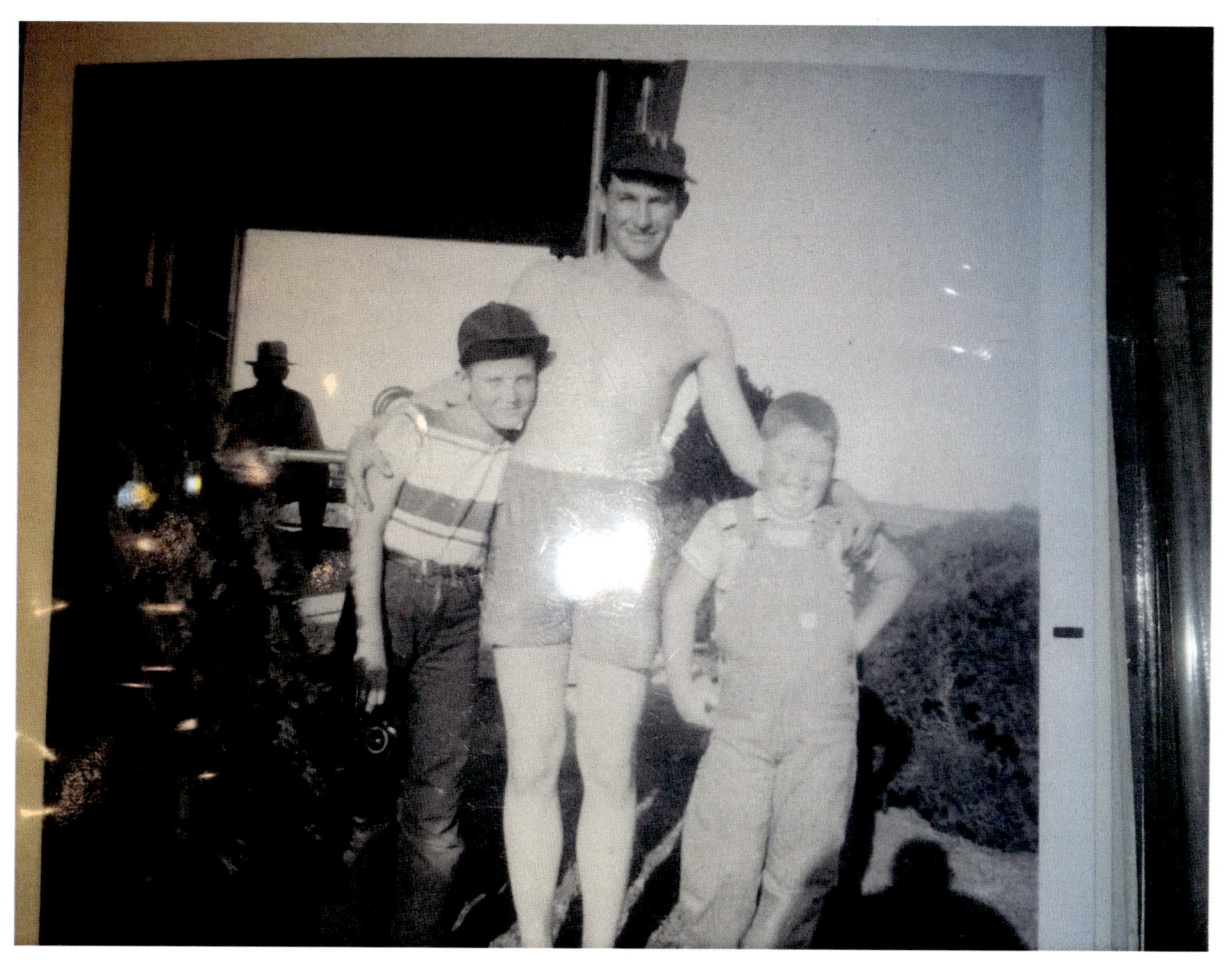

Richie, Harold, Bill Tamplen

INGREDIENTS

1 pound ground chuck, browned and drained
1 package Lawry's taco seasoning
2 cans ranch style beans
1 can whole corn
2 cans tomatoes (Ro-Tel if desired)
1 package ranch style dressing mix

STEPS

Brown ground chuck and drain, add package of Lawry's taco seasoning. Add all other ingredients. Heat and eat.

Makes 6 servings.

Spicy Tortilla Soup

Addie Ann Spicer Tamplen

INGREDIENTS

1 medium onion, chopped
1 jalapeno pepper, chopped
2 cloves garlic, minced
2 tablespoons oil
2 pounds stew meat
1 can 14 ½ ounce tomatoes
5 ounces Ro-Tel tomatoes with green chilies
1 can 10 ½ ounces beef broth
1 can 10 ¾ ounces tomato soup
1 ½ cans 10 ¾ ounces tomato soup of water
1 teaspoon ground cumin
1 teaspoon chili powder
1 teaspoon salt
½ teaspoon lemon pepper seasoning
2 teaspoons Worcestershire sauce
3 tablespoons tabasco sauce
4 tortillas, cut in 1-inch squares
¼ cup grated cheddar cheese

STEPS

Sauté first 5 ingredients in large pot. Add remining ingredients except tortilla and cheese. Simmer for 50 minutes. Add tortillas and cook for 10 minutes. Pour into bowls and sprinkle cheese on top. Spicy but good.

Makes 8 servings.

Tortilla Soup

Addie Ann Spicer Tamplen

INGREDIENTS

6 14 ½ ounce cartons chicken broth
2 4-ounce cans chopped mild green chilies, undrained
1/3 cup fresh mint leaves
2 cloved minced garlic
1 teaspoon chili powder
1 teaspoon ground cumin seed

Individual bowl ingredients
1 cup chopped fresh tomatoes
2 avocadoes, chopped
½ cup fresh cilantro
4 slices bacon, crumbled
3 cups tortilla chips, broken

STEPS

For soup, combine chicken brother, chilies, mint, garlic, chili powder, and cumin in Dutch oven. Bring to a boil Reduce heat.

Cover and simmer for 1 hour. Strain broth. Bring to a boil.

Combine other ingredients into bowls (1/4 cup). Ladle broth over garnish with sour cream.

Makes 12 servings.

OTHER

Barbeque Sauce

Dewayne and Kris Tamplen

INGREDIENTS

3 tablespoons butter or bacon fat
1 medium onion
2 tablespoons brown sugar
3 tablespoons Worcestershire sauce
1 cup water
2 tablespoons vinegar
1 cup catsup
1 tablespoon prepared mustard

STEPS

Sauté onion in bacon grease or butter. Mix all other ingredients with onion. Bring to boil. Simmer several minutes. If onion flakes or instant minced onions are used, bacon grease is not necessary.

Makes 6 servings.

Black Bean Salsa

Addie Ann Spicer Tamplen

INGREDIENTS

2 15-ounce cans black beans, rinsed and drained
1 17-ounce whole kernel corn, drained
2 large tomatoes, seeded and chopped
1 large avocado, peeled and chopped
1 purple onion, chopped
¼ cup chopped fresh cilantro
4 tablespoons lime juice
2 tablespoons olive oil
1 tablespoon red wine vinegar
1 teaspoon salt
½ teaspoon pepper

Garnishes: avocado slices, fresh cilantro

STEPS

Combine first 11 ingredients in a large bowl. Cover and chill. Garnish with cilantro and avocado. Serve with tortilla chips.

Makes 6 servings.

Campfire Chili

Brian K. Tamplen

Richie, Linda, Sandra, and Bill Tamplen

INGREDIENTS

2 pounds ground chuck
2 cans whole tomatoes, 14 ½ ounces, broken up
2 cans kidney beans, 15 ounces each
2 packages Chili seasoning

STEPS

Brown beef and drain fat.

Stir in chili seasoning, whole tomatoes (with juice) and kidney beans. Bring to a boil. Cover and simmer 10 minutes.

Makes 8 servings.

This recipe tastes great on a camping or hunting trip with a bunch of hungry campers.

Garlic Green Beans

Addie Ann Spicer Tamplen

INGREDIENTS

2 tablespoons olive oil
4 cups green beans
½ teaspoon salt and pepper
2 tablespoons vegetable bouillon
2 teaspoons mince garlic
½ teaspoon thyme
2 cups water

STEPS

Heat oil Add garlic and beans. Stir. Add thyme, salt, and pepper. Add water and bouillon. Bring to a boil. Cover. Simmer until beans are tender.

Makes 6 servings.

Green Pickled Tomatoes

Addie Ann Spicer Tamplen

INGREDIENTS

2 quarts sliced green tomatoes
3 tablespoons salt
2 cups red wine vinegar
2/3 cup dark brown sugar, firmly packed
1 cup sugar
3 tablespoons mustard seed
½ teaspoon celery seed
1 teaspoon ground turmeric
3 cups sliced yellow onions
2 large red bell peppers, chopped
1 large hot green or red pepper, chopped

STEPS

Mix tomatoes and salt. Let stand about 12 hours. Drain

Heat vinegar, sugar, and spices to a boil. Add drained tomatoes and pepper. Bring slowly to a boil. Simmer 5 minutes stirring with a wooden spoon.

Wash jars with soapy water and rinse.

Add jars and lids into water. Gradually bring to a boil. Boil for 20 minutes.

Pack hot jars with tomatoes. Be sure syrup covers vegetables. Adjust lids. Process in a boiling water (212 degrees) for 5 minutes. Remove jars and complete seals (turn tight) unless jars are self-sealing.

Makes 9 ½ servings.

Hot Salsa

Frankie Tamplen

Tyler, Bailey, Tad, Marci, Avery Ann, Randy, Frankie, Brian, Addie Ann, Harold, Krista, Kris, and Dewayne Tamplen

INGREDIENTS

2 quarts fresh tomatoes (after core-ing and quick boil to remove skins,, they will be soft and easy to measure)
10 fresh jalapeno peppers, chopped
¼ green bell pepper, chopped
1 medium onion, chopped
2 teaspoons white vinegar
2 teaspoons salt
1 teaspoon sugar
1 dash garlic salt
1 small can tomato sauce

STEPS

To skin tomatoes, place cored tomatoes into fresh boiling water for 3 – 4 minutes. Skins will split. Take tomatoes out and place into cold water. Slip skins off as soon as possible. Drain as much juice as possible.

Chop and place in food processor.

Put tomatoes and all other ingredients in a large pot and bring to a rolling boil. Boil for 25 minutes.

Prepare jars for canning.

Pour mixture into jars.

Do not fill to top. Wipe off edges and seal. Place into boiling water bath. Boil for 10 minutes.

Marinated Asparagus

Addie Ann Spicer Tamplen

Addie Ann Spicer and Brian Tamplen

INGREDIENTS

2 14 ½ ounce asparagus cans, drained
1 green pepper, chopped
1 bunch green onions with tops, chopped
¾ cup vegetable oil
½ cup red wine vinegar
½ cup sugar
½ clove garlic, minced
¼ teaspoon paprika
Pimento strips

STEPS

Place asparagus in shallow dish. Combine next 8 ingredients. Mix well and pour over asparagus. Chill 4 hours to overnight. Drain marinade before serving. Garnish with pimento strips.

Makes 8 servings.

Orange Vinaigrette

Addie Ann Spicer Tamplen

INGREDIENTS

1 quart orange juice concentrate
1 ½ cups strong Dijon mustard
1 ½ cups champagne wine vinegar
¾ gallon salad oil
1 tablespoon sesame oil
Salt and pepper
Water

STEPS

Blend orange juice, mustard, and half of the vinegar in mixer. Slowly drizzle in oil adding water to adjust thickness. Add vinegar if needed. Add sesame oil. Salt and pepper to taste. Adjust to ¼ size of recipe if needed.

Adjust recipe as necessary for smaller portions.

Makes 120 servings.

Red Chili Pepper Vinaigrette

Addie Ann Spicer Tamplen

INGREDIENTS

¼ cup sweet chili sauce
1/8 cup fish sauce (optional)
1 tablespoon cilantro, minced
1 cup water
¼ cup lime juice
2 tablespoons sugar
1 teaspoon ginger, minced (optional)
1 teaspoon garlic, minced (optional

STEPS

Mix all ingredients and chill until ready to use.

Makes 6 servings.

The Authors

Photo courtesy of Kolanowski Studio

Made in the USA
Columbia, SC
10 September 2024

7974b7da-a120-4f92-b1bc-2062aa5772e9R01